Practical Computer Skills for Social Work

WITHDRAWN

D0182648

000211613

Transforming Social Work Practice – titles in the series

To order, please contact our distributor: BEBC Distribution, Albion Close, Parkstone, Poole, BH12 3LL. Telephone: 0845 230 9000, email: learningmatters@bebc.co.uk. You can also find more information on each of these titles and our other learning resources at www.learningmatters.co.uk.

Practical Computer Skills for Social Work

CLAIRE GREGOR

Series Editors: Jonathan Parker and Greta Bradley

LearningMatters

Windows XP™ and Office XP™ © Microsoft Corporation, all rights reserved. Screen displays from Office XP™ and Windows XP™ are reprinted with permission from Microsoft Corporation.

First published in 2006 by Learning Matters Ltd.

All rights reserved. No part of this publication may be reproduced, stored in a retrieval system, or transmitted in any form or by any means, electronic, mechanical, photocopying, recording, or otherwise, without prior permission in writing from Learning Matters.

© 2006 Claire Gregor

British Library Cataloguing in Publication Data
A CIP record for this book is available from the British Library.

ISBN-10: 1 84445 060 0
ISBN-13: 978 1 84445 060 2

Cover design by Code 5 Design Associates Ltd
Project management by Deer Park Productions, Tavistock, Devon
Typeset by PDQ Typesetting Ltd
Printed and bound in Great Britain by Bell & Bain Ltd, Glasgow

Learning Matters Ltd
33 Southernhay East
Exeter EX1 1NX
Tel: 01392 215560
Email: info@learningmatters.co.uk
www.learningmatters.co.uk

Contents

List of activities

Acknowledgements

A big thank you goes to my colleagues and all social work degree students at Buckinghamshire Chilterns University College who road-tested the original version and contributed greatly to the development of this book. Their comments, suggestions, and tolerance have been invaluable. I would also like to thank my family, in particular my mother, a self-confused computer novice, who worked diligently through draft versions of the test. In addition, thanks go to Justin Luker in SCPE at BCUC who patiently helped me to gain my own ECDL qualification and who continues to be extremely supportive in my quest to become more IT literate.

I would also like to thank all my former colleagues in the CMHTs in Ipswich where I worked when I first qualified. Their unfailing encouragement and support in my professional development enabled me to move from being the 'Compass SuperUser' into academia.

Finally, I would like to thank Ali for his continued support and belief in me, and without whom I might still be staring at a blank computer screen.

Claire Gregor

Introduction

In the 1980s, or even as recently as the 1990s, you could be forgiven for wondering what on earth being able to use a computer had to do with your chosen profession of social work. However, nowadays with the accessibility of cheap, efficient and reliable technology, it is rare to find a desk in the Social Work office without a computer on it. If you work in one of the few remaining workplaces without a computer, you can reasonably expect that this *status quo* will be short-lived.

Shortly after its formation in 2003, the Social Care Institute for Excellence (SCIE) was commissioned by the Department of Health to 'assist the social care community [in making] the best use of information and communication technologies for teaching and learning, to deliver an improved service to users and carers' (DoH: 2003, cited in SCIE: 2003). Included within this drive was the General Social Care Council's requirement that all social work degree courses must assess to ensure that their graduates are computer literate to the level of the European Computer Driving Licence (ECDL) or its equivalent (2002). Therefore, if you are studying for a degree in social work, or indeed are already a qualified social worker with limited computer literacy, you will now need to take active steps to improve your computer skills. This book has been designed to help you do just that.

This book is divided into nine chapters linked to the following Microsoft applications:

- Windows Explorer
- Word
- Excel
- Access
- PowerPoint
- Outlook
- Internet Explorer

The aim of *Practical Computer Skills for Social Work* is to introduce you to the main concepts of modern computers as well as the main functions of commonly used software applications and how they interface with contemporary social work. Through a combination of conceptual information and practical exercises the book will give you the confidence and ability to use computers without fear as a qualified social worker.

Each chapter contains a 'getting started' section which will guide you through the basics and help to familiarise you with the software application. In order to ensure that the book is compatible with all versions of Microsoft Windows, all 'getting started' sections have screen dumps using the 'Classic' Windows screen format that is utilised by Windows 95, 98, 2000 and as an option by Windows XP. Following on from the introduction to the software, you will then find a number of practical activities designed to help you practise using the software. At the end of the book you will find model answers to the quiz questions and step-by-step guides on how to do each activity. Although the guides are based on Windows XP and Office XP, users of older versions should still be able to understand how to undertake the activities successfully.

You do not need to work through this book sequentially, but can dip in and out of it as suits you. The book has 50 activities in total so do all of them as in this way you can develop an impressive portfolio of material to demonstrate your computer literacy. This portfolio can be either in paper format, or as an electronic version to show your tutors or potential employers.

In order to assess your current level of ability and help you to get the most out of this book, complete the following questionnaire as it will help identify your IT strengths and learning needs. You will then be ready to embark on the rest of the activities in the book.

IT questionnaire

This is for you to complete to assess your previous use of computers and level of competence and to identify future learning needs. You may like to share with your tutor or IT department who will be able to advise you on how to meet your IT learning needs.

General computing experience

Please tick one of the following:
Do you use computers regularly?

I have never used a computer.	☐ (Please go to Q1)
I have used a computer once or twice.	☐ (Please go to Q2)
I use computers for specific purposes, i.e. only one or two programs but wouldn't know where to start with a new program.	☐ (Please go to Q3)
I have some computer knowledge and can use programs if shown.	☐ (Please go to Q4)
I consider myself computer literate and can use most programs with little help.	☐ (Please go to Q4)

1 For those who have never used a computer:

I have never used a computer because:

I have never had need to use a computer; *(please tick)*

But am confident I can do so if shown   ☐
And don't think I will be able to   ☐

I avoid them whenever possible;

But feel I could use one if I had to   ☐
As I feel they will be too difficult to learn to use   ☐

2 Limited use of computers:

Have you used a word processing program such as Microsoft Word? *(Please tick)*

No   ☐
A bit   ☐
Regularly   ☐

Do you use e-mail?

Yes ☐

No ☐

Have you used the Internet?

Yes, I am happy to browse the world wide web ☐

No, but I would like to learn ☐

No, I don't know how to. ☐

3 Some computing knowledge:

How would you describe your computing knowledge? *(Please tick)*

Own a computer and use regularly for word processing,
Internet and e-mail ☐

Own a computer but only use in a limited way ☐

Use a computer at work in a limited way ☐

4 Identifying computer knowledge:
(please delete as appropriate)

In computer terms, are you confident that you know:

How to launch an application from the Start menu? Yes/No

What a file and a folder are? Yes/No

Do you understand the difference between navigating within a program
and within the computer's operating system? Yes/No

Are you happy that you understand:

The difference between Internet Explorer and Windows Explorer? Yes/No

The difference between WindowsXP and OfficeXP? Yes/No

What a web browser is? Yes/No

What a URL is? Yes/No

How to find and save files on a flash drive and/or local hard drive? Yes/No

For those who have never used a computer

Talk to your IT department and see if they offer any taught classes which may well be provided free of charge. Alternatively, most local adult education colleges offer day and evening classes on basic computer skills for beginners. Lists of courses can usually be obtained from your local library. You can also sign up with LearnDirect, the government's low-cost adult education initiative (tel: 0800 100 900 or **http://catalogue.learndirect.co.uk/browse/usingit/**). If you prefer to teach yourself, there are lots of books on the market offering guides to software applications and at the end of the book you will find a list of some of the more popular titles. This book has been devised to offer you the basics to understanding and utilising many of the functions offered by Microsoft Word, Excel, Access, Powerpoint, Outlook and Internet Explorer. You will find model answers to all of the activities at the back of the book and can therefore use these to help increase your understanding of how each software package works. The book will therefore help you to become proficient in the main aspects of IT that you will need for social work.

For those who have limited or some knowledge of computers

You may already feel confident in the basics of Word and e-mailing, but feel a bit apprehensive about starting to use software packages such as Excel and Access. As above, you can sign up to specific classes to assist with increasing your skill in particular software packages, but this book will also guide you through the basics. One of the best ways to learn how to use new computer software is simply by practising and this often means making mistakes along the way! Look through the book and see if there are any activities that you already feel you could do and undertake these first to increase your confidence. Then move on to some of the more challenging activities and perhaps use the model answers at the back to help when you get stuck. Remember that each software package also comes complete with a 'Help' function that will be able to point you in the right direction if you are unsure how to carry out a specific task.

For those who already feel quite proficient in using computers

This book will help you to identify areas that you need to work on if you intend to actually sit the ECDL exam. Try undertaking all of the activities without looking at the model answers. By undertaking all of the activities you can build up an impressive portfolio of IT skills that you can present to your university tutor or potential employer in order to demonstrate your computer literacy and meet the qualifying requirements of the General Social Care Council.

Chapter 1
Social work and the computer

Many recent research studies into the role and tasks of contemporary social workers have identified that increasingly more working hours are taken up with administrative tasks (e.g. Lewis and Glennerster, 1996; Postle, 2002). This inevitably means that more working hours are spent in front of a computer than face to face with a service user. Hence, whilst you may possess empathic people skills and be adept at communicating orally, if you cannot find your way around a computer, you will find yourself struggling to achieve all of the functions required of you by your employer. In fact, it is now becoming the norm for job descriptions to include personal requirements such as:

- knowledge of financial and care management IT systems;
- experience of the preparation and presentation of reports across a range of related subject areas;
- exposure to IT facilities and systems associated with clients, budgets and management information.
  (Source: Hampshire County Council Senior Practitioner Job Description 2005)

As the ensuing chapters will hopefully illustrate, computers can be utilised in a wide variety of applications to assist not only the frontline social worker, but also staff in non-client contact roles such as senior managers and policy makers. However, even though the use of computers is now endemic in social work departments, it does not mean that individuals should not critically engage with the debates surrounding their use.

As Glastonbury wisely noted back in 1985:

> information is like money – once you hand it to someone else it is no longer yours, and all you can be reasonably sure about is that a little bit of it may be saved, but most will be passed on and eventually go into general circulation.

Case recording on service users' files offers a worrying practical illustration of this. In the days of paper files, the case file would sit in either the social worker's own filing cabinet or a communal office one. The only people who would have access to the handwritten notes within it were the social workers and administrative staff in that office and their immediate manager. In rare cases, the file may have been viewed by higher management, the legal department or an external auditor. After the case was closed the file would be sent to archives and then only retrieved if necessary for future work, or if the client had requested access. In modern social services, complex client databases have been set up and networked across service user groups. Therefore, information that has been recorded on a service user's file could potentially be accessed by multiple workers, for different purposes, raising all sorts of ethical dilemmas. It also allows for potential abuse of the system with users of the IT system having the opportunity to check out whether friends, neighbours or relatives are known to social services. What does this say of social workers' pledge to vulnerable service users that all information gathered on them will be held confidentially?

In a similar vein, e-mails are increasingly being used between social workers, their managers and other agencies in order to communicate about clients. Whilst this can be a very time-efficient way of gaining quick answers to queries, it can also result in service users' personal information being compromised. As with traditional post ('snail-mail'), e-mails can go astray and not arrive. If in a rush, an e-mail could inadvertently be sent to the wrong person, or the message could be misinterpreted by the recipient. As with all forms of communication, e-mail should be seen as an aid to communication, not the sole means at the expense of more personal contact such as the telephone or face-to-face dialogue.

The Data Protection Act 1998 and Freedom of Information Act 2000 are both pieces of legislation designed to give individuals some protection from information held on them electronically being misused. The Data Protection Act 1998 ensures that social care organisations manage the personal information they hold in a responsible way. They must ensure that information held is accurate and up to date, only kept for as long as required for a specified purpose, and kept secure (ICO, 2005). The Freedom of Information Act 2000 allows individuals to view records held by public authorities including social services and health authorities. Significantly, this Act allows individuals access not only to database records, but also e-mails and other electronic material relating to them. Social workers should therefore think twice before dashing off a quick informal e-mail to a manager or colleague about a service user. The e-mail could enter the public domain if the service user elected to exercise their legal rights to see information held on them. However, the legislation does offer an escape clause and access to case records remains subject to agreement from senior managers. Information may still legally be withheld if it is not felt to be in the client's best interests to view it (Brammer, 2003).

The Data Protection Act 1998 requires that all service users are aware that information on them is held electronically. As a frontline worker, it is arguably therefore the responsibility of the social worker to advise them of this. Clients of social services have always had the opportunity to request access to information held on files about them, and in the past this involved sitting with files of handwritten case notes. Although the files were often unwieldy, information such as letters from third parties could easily be removed if the author had not given consent for it to be viewed. This process could be a lot more complex if the majority of the case records are electronic and poses the dilemma of whether they should all be printed out as hard copy or whether the service user should be given access to a computer in order to read them.

> *Are you aware of your agency's policy on data protection and use of electronic resources? If not, try to locate it. How accessible is it? Is it available to service users as well as staff?*

All of the discussion thus far presupposes that the information held on social services computer systems is accurate, or, for case recording, at least a fair representation of the views of the social worker/service user/carer. However, research conducted by Glastonbury in 1995 (cited by Sapey, 1997) indicates that about one in four records held by social services departments contains inaccurate data. He offers the following reasons for this:

- too many links in the chain between the worker who interviews the service user and the eventual input of data;

- standardisation of complex information collected from the service user in order to ensure that it fits into 'boxes';

- information becoming quickly out of date on the system and not updated regularly enough;

- frontline workers (e.g. residential care staff, family centre workers, multi-disciplinary team workers) being more likely to use paper systems alongside IT.

Although this research is now over ten years old, it is reasonable to assume that the same issues are still relevant to social care.

At times it may feel as though social work values are incompatible with using a computer. This partly arises due to the outsourcing of social work specific program design to IT specialists rather than social work professionals. Whilst this outsourcing is clearly based on sound business principles of obtaining the most appropriate expertise for the job, it has resulted in data recording systems that dictate what a social worker can and cannot record, rather than vice versa. As Sapey (1997) suggests 'the use of information technology tends to be managed in a top-down and controlling manner'. It is therefore not surprising that social workers feel frustrated with the amount of time that they spend inputting data and filling in forms on the computer at the expense of face to face client contact (Postle, 2002).

Service user expectations (TOPSS England, 2002) highlight the skills and attributes that service users expect social workers to have. These do not specifically identify IT skills, but they do include:

- respecting confidentiality and informing users and carers when information needs to be shared about them;

- being honest about the power invested in them, including legal powers;

- putting users and carers first.

The case scenario below illustrates how the above expectations may not be met, albeit unintentionally, by the social worker who utilises the computer in order to record a referral:

CASE STUDY

Sara Pickering has had concerns for a while about her elderly neighbour Mrs Jacobs. Mrs Jacobs has been wandering down the street in the early hours in her nightwear and appears to be doing strange things. Sara rings up the local Social Services Referral Team and provides all of the relevant contact information for Mrs Jacobs, including the name of Mrs Jacobs' estranged daughter. Mrs Jacobs herself is unaware of the referral, and indeed has reassured Sara that she is fine. All of this information is entered into the computer system. The social worker entering the information notices that Sara already has an id. no on the system and is a client of the Learning Disability Team.

Can you identify what the issues are here?

You might have considered Mrs Jacobs' right to privacy and her lack of awareness that information was being recorded on a social services database without her knowledge. Mrs Jacobs is estranged from her daughter for a reason and may not appreciate her potentially being made aware of her situation. Similarly, Mrs Jacobs' daughter will now be unaware that social services holds information on her and may be very unhappy to find her name linked to her mother's case record. Sara rang social services in good faith, believing that she was passing on concerns about her neighbour. She may not have realised that the social worker entering the concerns could also access her own case records. The social worker may now perceive the referral differently as they may believe Sara to be an unreliable witness because of her learning disability. They may therefore contact the Learning Disability Team to speak to Sara's social worker, which is a consequence that Sara may never have anticipated. Sara's right to a private life is therefore also being violated.

The Computer Ethics Institute has formulated a handy checklist to bear in mind whenever utilising computers for either work or leisure, and it is essential for a social worker to have a basic awareness of the ethical implications of using a computer. The final 'commandment' is of particular relevance for social workers and links with the service user expectations mentioned earlier.

Ten Commandments of computer ethics

1. *Thou shalt not use a computer to harm other people.*
2. *Thou shalt not interfere with other people's computer work.*
3. *Thou shalt not snoop around in other people's computer files.*
4. *Thou shalt not use a computer to steal.*
5. *Thou shalt not use a computer to bear false witness.*
6. *Thou shalt not copy or use proprietary software for which you have not paid.*
7. *Thou shalt not use other people's computer resources without authorisation or proper compensation.*
8. *Thou shalt not appropriate other people's intellectual output.*
9. *Thou shalt think about the social consequences of the programe you are writing or the system you are designing.*
10. *Thou shalt always use a computer in ways that ensure consideration and respect for your fellow humans.*

Source: Computer Ethics Institute (1992)

Bearing each of the above commandments in mind, can you think of examples whereby a social worker or social care agency might break them?

Computers are incredibly powerful tools at the disposal of the social worker and, as the previous scenario demonstrated, service users may not even realise that they are being used to record information about them. In an ideal world all information held on computers about us would be accurate, but as Glastonbury's research (1995) illustrates, this is often not the case. False information could be maliciously entered into a computer and remain on an electronic record for years without us ever knowing.

One of the benefits of using a computer is that information can be processed and manipulated with minimum effort of the part of the operator. This can, however, have ethical implications. Imagine a situation whereby a social worker has forgotten to record an important meeting that took place a number of weeks previously. Depending on the software, the computer program may allow them to insert case notes into the service user's file that appear to be written at the time of the meeting. In reality they have been written some time after the event and therefore are subject to the memory recall of the social worker rather than being contemporaneous. Rather than acknowledging that they were at fault for not recording the meeting at the time, the social worker can pretend that they are up to date with their case recording, even though it may be inaccurate. However, it is worth bearing in mind that many programs contain advanced editing features that allow administrators to identify exactly when information was input.

Social care agencies typically employ large numbers of staff who all have access to complex databases that contain the confidential details of thousands of service users. These details can range from simple requests for Blue badges to allegations of child sexual abuse. The database may have different levels of access rights for staff in order to try to limit the potential for misuse of the information held within it. However, it is not difficult to imagine that individuals might be tempted to look up records to see whether their neighbours, family or friends are known to social services, thus abusing the service user's right to confidentiality.

The 'Ten Commandments' can also be interpreted as referring to information stored on the World Wide Web as well as within agencies or companies. Although information is freely available on the Internet, it is important to remember that this is also subject to copyright and the author needs to be acknowledged. Some local authorities have posted internal guidance on their web pages on how to complete various court reports. It can be tempting for other agencies to 'borrow' this material and simply change the logo or letterhead and claim the guidance as their own. This also applies to student essays that draw on information gleaned from the Internet. As with material found in books, all references must be fully sourced and traceable back to the original web page by providing a full URL (web address) as well as the date that the pages were accessed. Students should also be aware that software is now very sophisticated and packages are commercially available that allow lecturers to easily identify whether essay material has been plagiarised.

As a social worker you will generally be utilising generic programs such as Microsoft Office or a database package that has been purchased off the shelf by your employer. Occasionally a social care agency may commission a piece of software to undertake a more specific task. An example of this could be a program that holds all social workers' diaries centrally. Social workers could carry a palm-top computer to take with them on their visits and therefore book appointments using this. However, administrative staff based in the office could also book in appointments on behalf of the social worker. On one level this sounds like a very practical response to managing diaries. However, the information could be misused by the employer if they wish to monitor the movements of the social worker and check if they are using their time efficiently. The response of the social workers could ultimately be that they refuse collectively to use the software, as it is not being used for the purpose for which it was originally designed.

Chapter 2
Disability, health and safety issues

When personal computers were first developed, they were designed for right-handed users, with good motor control skills (e.g. use of their fingers) and good eyesight. Technology has moved on in leaps and bounds since the large commercial computers of the 1970s that required a large air-conditioned room and a team of specialists to work it. It is now possible to purchase a personal computer that is, or can be, specially adapted to your own personal needs. This may involve some financial outlay such as purchasing a keyboard guard to assist you with feeling the keys, or software such as voice recognition to reduce the need to type, as the computer is able to recognise the spoken word. If you think that you might benefit from having some specialised equipment to help you with using a computer, talk to the disability support services at your university or the personnel department at work as there may be a grant available to help with such costs.

Similarly you may be able to advise service users who use computers regularly at home who may not be aware of the potential for simple adaptations to make the computer easier to use. The Internet is an excellent tool to use to explore the various different computer-assisted technologies now available for people with disabilities. As a social worker it is vital to have an awareness of the different applications and this is very much in keeping with the social model of disability which is very empowering for individuals. Years ago, people were provided with grants in order to purchase telephones or wireless radios. Nowadays people are much more likely to wish to have a PC to communicate and keep up to date with what is happening in the world. With the gradual withdrawal of community services such as village post offices and mobile libraries, people living in rural communities and those who find it difficult to get out and about can benefit immensely from using a computer. This can help with everyday activities such as Internet banking, online shopping and information gathering and assist with individuals retaining their independence. Charities such as Aspire (**www.aspire.org.uk**) and Ability Net (**www.abilitynet.org.uk**) provide grants and helpful advice on their web pages about services and adaptations to computers for people with disabilities.

However, not all adaptations require specialist equipment. See below for some suggestions as to how an existing off-the-shelf computer could be adapted to make it more accessible and comfortable to use:

- The 'flash rate' of the cursor can be altered to slow it down if you find it too fast.
- The colour filters on the screen can be re-set in order to make text easier to see.
- 'Sticky Keys' can be created if you find it difficult to hold down more than two keys at a time, e.g. 'Control', 'Alt' and 'Delete'. This means that with just one key stroke you can carry out the same function.

- Visual alerts can appear on the screen every time your computer makes a noise alert.

- The keyboard response rate can be slowed if you have either hand or finger tremor so that it doesn't matter if your mis-hit other keys next to the one you wanted.

- The size of the icons (small pictorial symbols representing software or files) can be increased so that they are larger and easier to see.

- The mouse keys can be altered so that you can use the keypad arrows instead if you find using the mouse tiring.

- Different font sizes and styles can be used if you are visually impaired. RNIB recommends the use of fonts such as Arial 14pt.

- Documents can be printed onto different coloured paper. Many individuals with dyslexia find it easier to read typeface on pastel shades of paper. Using Comic Sans Serif font can also help as it is similar to handwritten script.

Activity 4.1 in Chapter 4 will help you to explore how to adapt your computer in the ways suggested above.

Remember as well to make sure that you do not sit for hours on end in front of the computer. As a general rule of thumb, get up and move around for 10 minutes in every hour. Pay attention to your posture when working and ensure that your back and wrists are well supported. Your seat should allow you to place both feet squarely on the floor. If this is not the case, you may need to acquire a footrest. Although it may be difficult to achieve in an office environment over which you have limited control, make sure that you work in a well-lit room without any glare on the screen. If you are copy-typing for long periods of time, you might also benefit from having a copy-holder which will position your work at eye level.

The checklist overleaf will help you to identify areas that you might need to address in order to work safely at your computer. If there are any aspects that you identify as requiring attention relating to a computer that you use at work, you need to flag this up with your Personnel department. Under Health and Safety Regulations, employers have a responsibility towards all employees who are regularly using computers as part of their work. The following two regulations are of particular relevance to social workers who increasingly spend a lot of time using computers:

- Management of Health and Safety at Work Regulations 1999. This requires that all employees are provided with adequate training when new technology is introduced. Therefore, local authorities must provide training when introducing new databases and recording systems to staff and cannot expect staff to simply learn as they go along.

- Health and Safety (Display Screen) Regulations 1999. This requires that every computer user must have a risk assessment carried out relating to their use of the computer. This includes an assessment of the workstation, location of the computer, and eyesight. Any findings from the assessment must be acted upon and appropriate equipment provided. If an employer does not provide either an assessment or equipment then they are in breach of health and safety legislation and could be prosecuted. Part of the assessment should include an eye test if you use the computer for the 'majority' of the day (this is not defined) and, if your eyesight is proven to have deteriorated as a result of using the computer, the employer should provide corrective glasses.

In addition, the Disability Discrimination Acts of 1995 and 2005 require employers to make 'reasonable adjustments' to employment conditions in order to support people with disabilities being able to carry out their jobs effectively. This includes providing adaptations to computer equipment if required. If you find that your employer is not honouring either health and safety legislation or the Disability Discrimination Acts, contact your union representative who should be able to direct you to a Union Health and Safety Officer. Alternatively, you could contact the government Health and Safety Executive (tel: 0845 345 0055 **www.hse.gov.uk**) for advice.

	Yes	No
A. Desk/Workstation		
1. Do you know how to adjust your workstation?	....	....
2. Have you arranged your workstation to meet your specific needs?	....	....
3. Is there space in front of the keyboard to support your hands and forearms?	....	....
4. Do you have sufficient leg room?		
5. Is your workstation and surrounding area free from obstruction and hazards?	....	....
6. Does most of your work require reading from hard copy documents?	....	....
7. If so, do you require a document holder?	....	....

	Yes	No
B. Posture		
1. Can you sit comfortably and easily change your posture?	....	....
2. Can you adjust your equipment to a comfortable viewing position?	....	....
3. Can you place your feet firmly on the floor?	....	....

	Yes	No
C. Display screen		
1. Is the information displayed on your screen clear and easy to read?	....	....
2. Can the brightness and contrast be adjusted easily?	....	....
3. Is the image on the screen stable and free from flicker?	....	....
4. Is your screen free from reflected glare?	....	....
5. Does the monitor swivel/move adequately in each direction?	....	....

	Yes	No
D. Keyboard		
1. Is the keyboard separate from the screen?	....	....
2. Can the tilt of the keyboard be altered/adjusted?	....	....
3. Are the key symbols easy to read?	....	....
4. Does the keyboard have a matt surface to avoid reflected glare?	....	....

	Yes	No
E. Chair		
1. Is the chair comfortable and can the height and backrest be adjusted?	....	....
2. Can all adjustments be made easily and safely?	....	....

	Yes	No
F. Lighting		
1. Has your computer been situated to avoid direct glare?	....	....
2. Does the lighting allow you to work comfortably?	....	....

(Adapted from BCUC Health and Safety Checklist, 2005)

Chapter 3
Basic concepts of information technology

At first glance, you may think that this chapter is too technical and might be tempted to skip it, believing that it has no relationship to your practice as a social worker. However, as the previous section on social work and computers has already discussed, the use of IT in the social care sector is fraught with issues relating to confidentiality, data protection and file security. Many people now work at home in order to complete complex reports in time for court hearings and confidential information may be saved on their home PC or laptop. It is vital to be aware of the implications of having your laptop stolen, or another family member having access to client files, albeit inadvertently. Only by having an awareness of computer security as opposed to home or office security can you take steps to protect your and your clients' information. You probably don't think twice about making sure that paper files are locked up in a filing cabinet before you leave the office. The same level of security should be applied to electronic files.

Whilst you may have access to an IT helpdesk at work, this service is not always available and many queries can often be simply resolved if the user has a basic awareness of how the computer works. What would you do if your computer crashed and you needed to access vital information for a last-minute meeting relating to the protection of a vulnerable client? Having an awareness of how the computer stores and processes information can help to minimise the risk of crises such as this.

What is a personal computer?

It is very difficult to describe in simple terms exactly what a personal computer is as it does not have a specific function, unlike a washing machine, for example, that does have a very well-defined function, i.e. to wash clothes. The *Oxford English Dictionary* defines a computer as:

> *a usually electronic device for storing and processing data (usually in binary form), according to instructions given to it in a variable program*

This is a somewhat inaccessible definition and contains a number of concepts that are not immediately obvious, e.g. 'binary form', 'variable program'. In order to really understand what a computer is, it is necessary to move beyond a simplistic definition and explore the subject in more depth.

Personal computers, or PCs, are essentially general-purpose machines and their function depends on what application (program) the person operating the computer chooses to carry out (run). For example, if the operator runs a word processing application on the computer, the function of the computer becomes that of a very powerful typewriter. Similarly, if the operator runs a web browser such as Internet Explorer, the computer becomes a machine that allows the user to access the Internet.

The physical components that make up a computer are called 'hardware' and this term can be applied to the keyboard, screen and printer. Programs or applications that can be run on a computer are what is known as 'software'. Figure 3.1 depicts a personal computer in its most basic form.

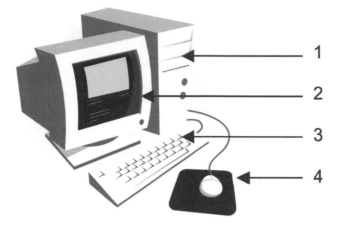

Figure 3.1

To operate the computer, the user will utilise the mouse (4) and keyboard (3) in order to input commands or data into the computer. The base unit (1) will then carry out or 'process' the command and then output the results on the visual display unit (2). Another way of thinking about this is to imagine the computer in the visual terms depicted in Figure 3.2.

Figure 3.2

The *input* would be typing 'Hello' using the keyboard. The base unit would *process* the information received from the keystrokes and then *output* the results as 'Hello' displayed on the screen. All inputs received into the computer, whether a click of the mouse button, key strokes or the spoken word into a microphone, are converted into numerical binary code and processed in calculations performed at a rate of many millions per second. The results of the calculations can then be output in a variety of forms such as sound via a loudspeaker, or text or graphics on a screen or printer.

In order for the base unit to operate, it requires certain building blocks or components. In addition to the power supply, a base unit will typically contain a 'motherboard' and disk drives as a bare minimum. The motherboard is an electronic circuit board which contains the microprocessor, memory and connectors for connecting peripheral devices (e.g. keyboard, mouse and printer) and disk drives. Most modern motherboards also contain circuitry to generate sounds and video output signals to the visual display unit. Older motherboards required extra boards known as 'daughter cards' connected to them in order to generate sounds and video signals. The electronic circuit board that generates sound is often referred to as a 'sound card' and plugs into connectors on the motherboard in order to enhance its functionality. However, these days most of these cards are already built into the motherboard.

The microprocessor on the motherboard is the 'brains' of the computer and this is known as the 'central processing unit' or CPU. Its job is to carry out or execute commands and perform calculations. The speed at which it is able to do this is a measure of how powerful (and often expensive) the computer is. The microprocessor's clock speed, measured in MHz or GHz, is an indicator of how many calculations the microprocessor can execute per second. The clock speed of the microprocessor is therefore used as a way of quantifying how much processing power is available to the user and you will often see PCs marketed on the basis of the speed of the microprocessor. Many computer advertisements also mention the microprocessor separately by name, e.g. Intel Pentium 4.

In order to carry out the calculations mentioned above, the microprocessor requires 'memory'. Memory is where the microprocessor stores the data on which it needs to carry out mathematical operations. There are two types of memory on the motherboard: RAM and ROM. RAM or random access memory is used by the microprocessor to store data that it needs to carry out its calculations. It is like a piece of scrap paper that you might use in an exam to work out rough calculations. Once you have completed your rough calculations and no longer need them, you erase them from the scrap piece of paper so that you can use the paper for the next set of rough calculations. RAM is only capable of storing data whilst it is supplied with power and therefore once the computer is switched off, it loses all its information. ROM or read-only memory, on the other hand, maintains its information even when the power is switched off. Personal computers typically have very little ROM and the only thing that ROM is used for is to store the initial start-up information that the microprocessor needs to operate. This includes information such as where the printer port is, how many disk drives are connected to the motherboard and where to look for and execute the 'operating system'.

When referring to the memory capacity of a computer, it is always in terms of how much RAM it has, not how much ROM. The amount of memory that a computer has significantly affects how fast the computer can operate – hence it being a selling feature of the PC. The memory is measured in 'bytes' and therefore the more bytes, the more memory the computer has.

Imagine that you need to do numerous calculations and only have one scrap of paper. Every time your piece of paper is filled up, you need to erase all of the calculations and then start using the paper again. This takes time. However, if you had two pieces of scrap paper you could do twice as many calculations before you needed to stop and rub the rough calculations out. By the same token, if your computer has more memory, it can do more calculations before it has to stop and erase them, and therefore it will generally run applications or programs faster. However, it is important to note that increasing the amount of memory will not necessarily increase the speed of the processing indefinitely as there are other factors that impact on the processing speed.

When you run a program the microprocessor will execute the code and store the necessary parts in RAM. The computer will then behave like the machine that the program intends, e.g. a word processor. When you have written a letter, for example, you may wish to save it for a later date. You would not save it in RAM because as soon as you switched off the computer, it would be lost. Even if you could save it in ROM, there is not enough spare capacity in your personal computer to save even the shortest letter. Therefore, you have to save it to a disk drive.

Disk drives are mass storage devices that are used to store your programs and files. The hard disk stores programs and files, including the 'operating system', for an indefinite period of time. The operating system is a program that is always run when you turn on the computer and an example of one is Windows XP. It allows the user to control the functions of the computer utilising a user-friendly interface. Without the operating system the user would have to resort to interacting with the computer by inputting binary code. Unlike RAM, disk drives store information even when the power supply is switched off and therefore are ideal for storing data such as the operating system, letters, spreadsheets, and databases. As with RAM and ROM, the amount of information that a 'disk' can store is measured in bytes. There are a number of different types of disk drives that you may come across and each has a different amount of storage capacity:

- Floppy – 1.4 Megabytes (almost obsolete now)
- Hard disk – up to 1000 Gigabytes
- CD-ROM – 800 Megabytes
- DVD – 5.2 Gigabytes
- USB Pen/Flash – variable up to 1 Gigabyte (this is an external drive)

Out of all of the above drives, the best place generally to save your work is to the hard disk as data stored here can be accessed fastest. However, this means that files are stored just on the specific computer, and unless saved elsewhere in addition, they cannot be easily shared. Additionally you run the risk of losing your work if the hard disk fails. CD-ROM and DVDs are usually used for long-term archiving, and pen drives are extremely portable devices that are ideal for storing work on that needs to be shared or worked on in multiple locations (such as college work).

Another place where you can store work is on a 'network drive' if your computer is part of a network. This is likely if you are using a computer in an office. A network can consist of two or more computers and enables the users to share documents, e-mails and peripheral devices such as printers. There are two types of network: LAN (Local Area Network) and WAN (Wide Area Network). LANs typically connect computers within a single office building or small area and require special cabling in order to link the computers together. A WAN can connect computers over a wider area and utilises existing telephone networks and can therefore connect computers internationally. The Internet is essentially a network that connects millions of computers all over the world and to access it your computer needs to be connected to the telephone network via a device called a modem.

Glossary of terms

Like social work, IT is full of jargon and acronyms that can appear quite intimidating at first sight. Below you will find a list of the most commonly used terms along with explanations of what they mean. As you become more confident using the computer, many of these terms will become familiar everyday language for you.

Application	Software written for a specific purpose such as word processing
Bug	Defect in computer programming that causes a problem in the operation of either the computer or a piece of software
CPU	Central processing unit
Cursor	Flashing character that appears on the screen to indicate where data can be entered next
Data	Information, whether text or characters
GUI	Graphical user interface
Hard drive	Data storage area contained within the computer
Hardware	Mechanical equipment and components that make up a computer
Megabyte	Computer memory and hard disk space is measured using a binary system of **bits** and **bytes**. 8 bits = 1 byte, 1024 bytes = 1 kilobyte, therefore 1024 kilobytes = 1 megabyte
Modem	Device that enables the computer to connect to the Internet via the telephone network
Network	Two or more computers connected together in order to provide shared resources, e.g. files or printer
Peripheral device	Piece of hardware attached to computer, e.g. printer, keyboard, mouse
Processor	Part of the main computer that is responsible for analysing and processing the data.
RAM	Random access memory
ROM	Read-only memory
Scanner	Peripheral device that is able to scan letters and other documents so that they can be manipulated on screen and incorporated in other documents
Server	A powerful computer that holds data to be shared over a network of other computers
Software	Computer programs
Soundcard	Additional piece of hardware that can be plugged into the main part of the computer (motherboard) to enable sound to be produced
Terminal	Computer that is part of a networked system
USB	Universal serial bus – external port on the base unit that allows peripheral devices (see above) to be connected.
VDU	Visual display unit, otherwise known as the screen
Virus	Dangerous code that can irretrievably damage the data on your computer

Now have a go at the following activity to test your knowledge of some of the basic concepts of IT and how they interface with social work.

Activity **3.1**   *Computer quiz*

1. In local authority departments computers are often networked. Give three reasons why this has advantages for service users and staff.

2. What is the reason for using a password on a computer? Why do you see ***** when you type in your password?

3. Name a common desktop publishing application and explain its purpose and how you might utilise it as a social worker.

4. Explain the purpose of keeping backup copies of files.

5. Name two sources of computer viruses. What steps can you or your agency IT department take to reduce the risk of catching viruses?

6. What is the main purpose of the Data Protection Act? How does this apply to social care organisations?

7. How does system software differ from application software? Give one example of each.

8. Name five ways in which you might use a computer at home.

9. What does the acronym GUI stand for and what is GUI? Give two advantages of GUI compared with earlier methods of working with computers.

10. Name three different methods of communicating utilising the telephone network. Which of these methods requires the use of a computer?

11. What kinds of drive might you find attached to a computer?

12. Give two reasons for using pen drives to store files.

13. Which five steps can you take to ensure that you work in physical safety with your computer?

14. List three ways in which a local authority might use computers in order to improve the delivery of social care.

15. What is a CPU? How is its operating speed measured?

16. In what ways can a floppy diskette be accidentally damaged?

17. Give three reasons why social care organisations now use e-mail rather than the post for sending messages.

18. Explain the difference between 'dumb' and 'intelligent' terminals found on a networked computer system.

19. What is a common name for a portable computer? Describe three ways in which it differs from a desktop computer.

20. List two input and two output devices in a computer system. Select one output device and describe briefly how it works.

Chapter 4
Using a computer and managing files

Ask any member of the administrative team what the key elements to successfully locating information within the office are and their response is bound to include 'an efficient filing system'. The same applies to your computer. If you regularly type up your own reports and letters there is nothing more frustrating than being unable to locate them the next time you switch on your computer. The operating system allows you to create folders and directories within your own personal drive which can save time and frustration and prevent unnecessary telephone calls to the IT helpdesk. Similarly, by learning how to utilise the 'task manager' within the operating system you will be able to close down the one piece of software that has frozen, rather than always having to resort to reaching for the 'off' switch.

It is important to learn about the 'desktop' environment of your operating system as this enables you to personalise your PC with screensavers, larger icons, different colour schemes, etc. The desktop is the starting point for all applications that you run on a personal computer and therefore it is necessary to familiarise yourself with it and its full functions. You are able to access something known as the 'Control Panel' from the desktop which is invaluable if you have any form of visual impairment or dyslexia. In addition, learning about the Control Panel is essential as this is where you go if you wish to install additional hardware such as a new printer, or additional software such as a voice-recognition package.

Getting started

This chapter moves on from learning theoretically how a computer works to the practical aspects of using a modern PC or laptop. Depending on the age of your computer, you may be using different versions of Microsoft Windows operating system and Office at home, work and college. They all have the same common functions, but the later versions will be generally more user-friendly.

After your computer has been switched on, you will see what is known as the 'Desktop' appear on your screen. If you are using a computer at work or college, you may need to enter a username and password first before you are directed to the desktop. The default option consists of small pictures known as 'icons' arranged on either a blue screen or a pictorial background. You may also see a row of smaller icons at the bottom of the screen with a 'Start' button in the left-hand corner and a clock in the opposite one. This row is called the 'Taskbar'. If you click once on the 'Start' button, a menu will pop up and this is available to you irrespective of what program you subsequently choose to work on. You can select which program you wish to start, e.g. Word, or you can select an individual file, e.g. an essay you have already started working on.

You will need to work from the Desktop when you wish to make adjustments to your computer or organise your files. A computer works in a very structured and organised way. A 'file' is the name given to a particular piece of work that you are doing within a software application, e.g. an essay, a spreadsheet or database. These are then organised within 'folders' in order to make retrieving them easier. The folders are then saved within disk drives which may be integral to your computer, or external (see previous chapter). Figure 4.1 demonstrates how you might organise or locate a particular piece of work within your computer:

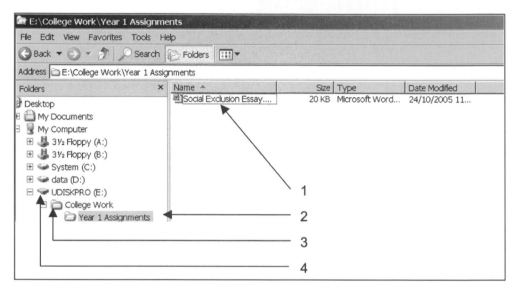

Figure 4.1

If you look in the 'Address Bar' you will see the address or location of the Word document 'Social Exclusion Essay'. You can see the document within the main pane of Windows Explorer (1). The document has been saved in the E disk drive (4), in the overall folder called 'College Work' (3), and then in a further sub-folder called 'Year 1 Assignments' (2).

There are two main areas where you can organise your files: Windows Explorer and My Computer. Figure 4.1 above is from Microsoft Windows Explorer. You can access this by double-clicking on the icon shown in Figure 4.2 on your Desktop:

Figure 4.2

Alternatively, you can access it via the 'Start' menu where it is hidden away within 'Programs' and then 'Accessories'. You will then see two 'panes' with the left-hand side showing where your folders are located within your computer. If you click on any folder in the left pane, you will see that the contents of that folder will appear in the right-hand pane. You can delete, copy, move and rename files within Windows Explorer.

'My Computer' works in a similar way and can be accessed by double-clicking on the icon shown in Figure 4.3 on your Desktop.

Figure 4.3

By double-clicking on the particular drive that you wish to search, all of the folders and files contained within that drive will be revealed.

The other main working area of the computer that you need to become familiar with is called the 'Control Panel' which is located within 'Settings' under the 'Start menu'. This is where you can alter various settings on your computer such as changing the size of icons, the click-speed of the mouse or you can add a screensaver here. You can also add additional hardware devices such as printers and install new software.

The activities within this chapter are designed to help you practise using both Windows Explorer and the Control Panel as well as to navigate your way around the Windows system from within other software applications that you may be using. As many of the activities are difficult to demonstrate to other people unless they are physically with you, you need to be able to create 'screen dumps'. A 'screen dump' will show what is on your screen at a given moment in order to evidence completion of the activity. To create a screen dump hold down the 'Ctrl' + 'Print Screen' button (this is generally on the top right of your keyboard). This will save a copy of the screen onto a virtual 'clipboard' for editing purposes. You are then able to paste a copy of the screen into another file such as a Word document or PowerPoint presentation. You can either use the shortcut 'Ctrl' + 'V' or the 'Paste' icon to do this. Your screen dump can be cropped using the Picture Toolbar if you wish, but for the purposes of these activities, you do not need to do this.

Have a go now at Activities 4.1–4.8.

Activity 4.1   *Using the Control Panel*

1. *From the desktop, access the Control Panel and carry out the following alterations to your computer:*

   a. *Create a visual alert every time that your computer makes a sound.*

   b. *Alter the blink rate of the cursor so that it does not blink and is static.*

   c. *Alter the width of the cursor so that it is wider.*

   d. *Change the resolution of the display screen so that it is high contrast.*

2. *Open up Word and type in some text in order to check if the alterations have been applied.*

Activity 4.2 — Using the Task Manager

1. Open up Word. Then downsize the application so that it appears as an icon on the bottom toolbar of your screen.

2. Open up Excel and do the same (don't worry if you do not have any personal spreadsheet files that you are working on – this activity can be done just by opening the program).

3. Open up your e-mail program as if you were going to work on it. You should now have three software applications running concurrently and will have three icons visible at the bottom of the screen, as in Figure 4.4.

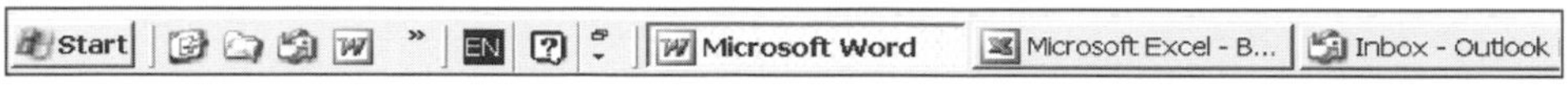

Figure 4.4

3. Now imagine that your screen has frozen and you are unable to send or receive e-mails or even type anything onto the screen. Open up the Task Manager.

4. Create a screen dump to illustrate your ability to access the Task Manager – this will show the box that pops up onto your screen indicating which programs are running. It should show the three programs all still running.

5. After you have created the screen dump, close down Excel and your e-mail program from within the Task manager.

Activity 4.3 — File management

1. Log on to Word and open up a piece of work that you have worked on recently. This could be on your 'personal' drive at college, on a USB pen-drive, or at home. Insert a header or footer to the document that includes the file directory, e.g. C:\My Documents\Application for Job.doc.

2. If you have not already created a folder for this piece of work, resave it in a new folder called 'IT Skills Portfolio' so that you can keep all of your IT work together and easily accessible.

3. Now print out the work, ensuring that you have a header or footer indicating the new file directory where the document has been saved.

Activity 4.4 — Navigating your computer

You will need to have a computer turned on in order to work through this exercise. Please provide as full an answer as possible (e.g. from the main Desktop screen, click on the 'Start' menu, then select the option 'Help', etc).

1. *In order to minimise the risk of losing unsaved data on your computer, what is the best way to shut down your computer after a session using Word?*

2. *Describe how you would go about resizing the window using your mouse.*

3. *What is the name of the program that you would use to shut down an application that has frozen? What key combination do you use to access it?*

4. *Where would you find the exact specification of your computer, e.g. the size of the microprocessor, amount of RAM? What is the specification of the computer you are using?*

5. *Where on the 'Start' menu would you go in order to alter the screensaver?*

6. *Which files have the following extensions?*
   a. *.doc*
   b. *.jpg*
   c. *.xls*
   d. *.pdf*

7. *Does your computer have more than one printer that it recognises? What is the name of the default printer? If there is more than one printer, what is the other printer called? How would you make this the default printer?*

8. *How would you change the rate at which the cursor blinks?*

9. *What software is contained in your computer's accessories folder?*

10. *How would you save a file to your Desktop? How would you know that you had carried this out successfully?*

Activity 4.5 — Creating sub-folders

1. *Open up Windows Explorer and locate your IT Skills folder (if you didn't create one in the previous activity, do so now).*

2. *Create new sub-folders for each of the chapters in this book: Basic concepts, Using a computer, Word processing, Spreadsheets, Databases, Presentations, Internet and Email.*

3. *Create a screen dump of the contents of your IT Skills folder from Windows Explorer to demonstrate that you have been able to create the sub-folders.*

Activity 4.6   *File management using Windows Explorer*

1. Open up a Word document and create a new document called 'File Management'. Make sure that you save it, then exit from Word.

2. Open up Windows Explorer and locate your document. Create a screen dump to demonstrate its current location.

3. Now move it to a different folder, preferably your IT Skills portfolio folder. If you have already saved it here, you will need to demonstrate that you can move it else where.

4. Rename the document 'Activity 4.6'.

5. Create another screen dump to demonstrate that you have done this. Note the time in the right-hand corner, and if you have completed the activity successfully, you will see that within approximately two minutes you should have been able to create a new folder.

6. If you have already undertaken some of the activities within this book, organise them now into the relevant sub-folder.

Activity 4.7   *Creating shortcuts on the desktop*

1. Insert a CD-ROM into your computer and ensure that your computer has recognised it. If you do not have a CD-ROM available, you can use a music CD.

2. Using the 'Start' menu, create a shortcut to the CD-ROM or other peripheral device so that when your computer is first switched on, you can go directly to it via the 'Start' menu. It should now appear as an option in the Start-up menu. See Figure 4.5.

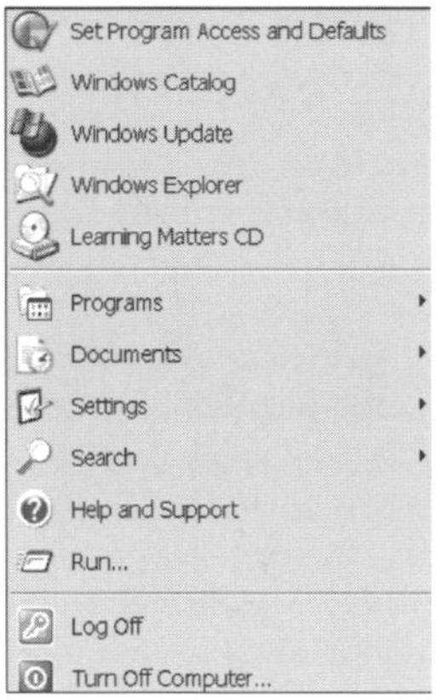

Figure 4.5

3. Copy this shortcut to the Desktop so that it appears as an icon on your screen.

4. Copy it additionally so that it appears on the Toolbar at the bottom of your screen. You should now be able to click on either icon and open up your CD-ROM or music CD directly without having to go into the relevant software application first to open up files that you wish to work on.

5. Create a screen dump with the 'Start' menu revealed to demonstrate your ability to do this.

Activity 4.8   *Using the print queue*

1. Open up a document in Word that you have recently been working on.
2. Turn off your printer if you already have it switched on. Now click on the 'Print' icon.
3. Open up another document in Word, but instead of clicking on the shortcut 'Print' icon use the pull-down menu to select 'Print'. Depending on the type of printer that you have, alter the format of your printed output in one of the following ways:

   a. Add the watermark 'Confidential' to your document.

   b. Print two pages to a sheet of paper.

   c. Print your document in landscape view.

4. You should now have two documents with different print formats in your Print Queue waiting to print once your printer is switched on. See Figure 4.6.

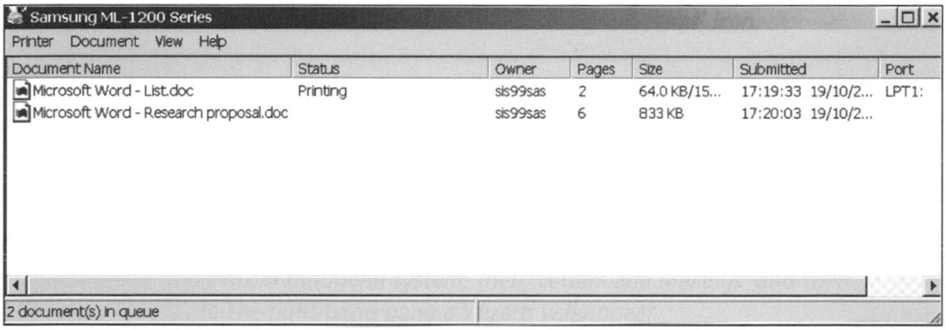

Document Name	Status	Owner	Pages	Size	Submitted	Port
Microsoft Word - List.doc	Printing	sis99sas	2	64.0 KB/15...	17:19:33 19/10/2...	LPT1:
Microsoft Word - Research proposal.doc		sis99sas	6	833 KB	17:20:03 19/10/2...	

Samsung ML-1200 Series — Printer Document View Help — 2 document(s) in queue

Figure 4.6

5. Switch on your printer and pause the first print job via the print queue (e.g. in the example above, pause the printing of 'List.doc') and select the second print job to commence.
6. Now delete the first print job entirely. Print out your second print job with the different format and put the hard copy in your IT Skills folder.

Chapter 5
Word processing

Many people are familiar with word processing and have no difficulty in conceptualising why it is important for social workers. Increasingly a social care administrator's time is taken up with budgetary matters and managing databases, leaving individual social workers to type their own letters and reports. Whilst there is no requirement by the GSCC to be able to touch-type, it certainly is a valuable skill to have! Familiarity with word processing software is not just restricted to text, but also includes being able to insert pictures or other computer-generated images or files. Whilst this would not be appropriate to include in a formal document such as a court report, it can add greatly to the accessibility and user-friendliness of other word-processed pieces such as Life Story books or posters. Additionally, when working with children or individuals with learning disabilities, it is sometimes helpful to contextualise written documents with pictures or symbols in order to facilitate communication.

One of the key social work skills is communication, and it is important to be mindful of the fact that much of a social worker's communication on behalf of a service user is undertaken using a computer. Word-processed reports and letters are daily activities for social workers and a means of interacting with both service users and other professionals. Therefore, a poorly executed document can reflect badly not only on the social worker but also on the service user. Having an awareness of basic presentation skills such as spell checking, aligning margins and the use of headings is essential. How would you view a doctor's letter if it contained numerous spelling mistakes and was grammatically incorrect? It probably would not inspire confidence! By being able to include headers and footers as well as page numbers, long documents can become less unwieldy and your documents will become a lot more accessible to the reader.

Word processing software has the additional benefit of being accessible for people with disabilities. Voice-recognition software can be installed which will translate the spoken word into text on the screen. This requires a bit of getting used to, but is an invaluable aid for people who find it difficult to use a keyboard. As a social worker you will be aware that the local authority is required to produce service plans in user-accessible formats including video, Braille and large-print. Use of the latter should be considered for letters to service users with visual impairments or dyslexia. This requires minimal expertise on the part of the computer user to alter the size and style of the font to make it easier to read (see also Chapter 2).

Getting started

There are many word processing packages available commercially such as WordPerfect, AmiPro or Lotus Word Pro. For the purposes of the ECDL you need to be proficient in Microsoft Word. This is accessed via the icon shown in Figure 5.1.

Figure 5.1

Most of the main functions that you will need to learn about in Word can be accessed from the toolbar at the top of the screen (Figure 5.2).

Figure 5.2

Word is a relatively straightforward software application to use and basic documents can be created without much knowledge of the program. Once you have double-clicked on the Word icon, or selected it from 'Programs' in the Start menu, you will be taken straight to a blank document called 'Document 1'. The cursor will flash in the top left of the screen and you are ready to go.

One of the most important things to remember when you are using Word is to save your work regularly. There is nothing more frustrating than spending hours on a report or assignment only to have all of your hard graft wiped out by a power cut. To save your work, you can either click on the 'Save' icon on the toolbar that resembles a floppy disk, or go to the 'File' pull-down menu and select 'Save'. If you haven't already decided on a name for your document, you will need to select 'Save As' and this allows you not only to name your document, but to decide where you wish to save it, e.g. you can specify which folder and drive you want to use to store the document.

Word processors have gained popularity over typewriters because of their enhanced ability to manipulate text. By using the 'Cut', 'Paste' and 'Copy' icons on the toolbar, or accessing the functions via the 'Edit' pull-down menu, you can reorganise the order of your typed material. In order for these functions to work, you have to have highlighted the words, paragraphs or phrases that you wish to move or copy. To do this you need to position the cursor over the first letter by clicking with the mouse. If you then hold down the left-hand mouse key and drag the mouse over the text you wish to move, you will see it becomes highlighted until you release the mouse button. The highlighted text can then be edited as you wish and gets sent to a 'virtual clipboard'. The text can either be completely 'cut' (deleted), copied or 'pasted' (removed from its existing place in the document and added in elsewhere) depending on which function you select. A shortcut for selecting the relevant option is to right-hand click on the mouse when the text is highlighted. A box will then appear as in Figure 5.3.

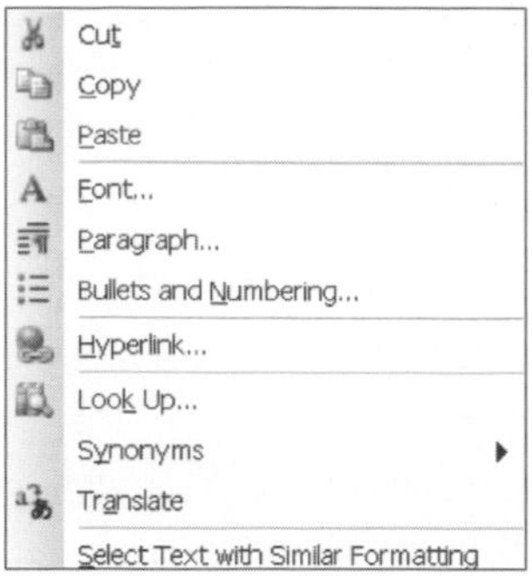

Figure 5.3

To insert or paste the text elsewhere, select the relevant option, move the cursor to the text's proposed new location and then left-click again with your mouse.

This box can also be used to alter the appearance of your text when it is highlighted. You can change the font from 'normal' to '**bold**' or '*italic*' or you can change the size or style of the text. You can also alter the paragraph spacing in this way. Alternatively, you can select the 'Format' pull-down menu and access these options from there.

Word also has the capacity to support pictures, photos and other graphic images imported from other programs. In order to insert images, select the 'Insert' pull-down menu and then select 'Picture' and you will be offered a variety of different options. The image will then be pasted into your document where your cursor is positioned. You can also use the 'Insert' pull-down menu to add page numbers or page breaks into your document.

The 'Tools' pull-down menu contains many helpful functions for essay writing. These include a spell-checker and a word count function. The spell-check feature is also available from an icon on the toolbar. In order to check your document, you can either highlight individual words that you are unsure of and the spell check will offer you alternative spellings or you can check the entire document. Whilst the spell check is a sophisticated tool, it cannot always pick up on the misuse of words such as 'their' instead of 'there' and you therefore cannot completely eliminate the need for careful proofreading.

Many of these functions also can be accessed via the icons in the toolbar below the menu. Spend some time familiarising yourself with these shortcut icons as they will save you a lot of time. Perhaps the most helpful icon to be aware of is the one shown in Figure 5.4.

Figure 5.4

On older versions of Word this icon helps you to undo your last action. However, more recent versions allow you to undo multiple actions. This can be extremely helpful when you realise that you have made a mistake and start panicking that you will never be able to recover your previous version.

Have a go now at Activities 5.1–5.8 that cover a variety of different aspects of Word and should increase your confidence and competence in using it.

Activity *5.1*   *Word processing and using shortcut keys*

1. *Open Word and create a blank document entitled 'Initial Learning Profile'.*
2. *Type in the following headings (without bullet points):*

   - *My social work (or related) background is:*
     Describe any previous social work experience, whether voluntary or paid.

   - *What I have learned from these experiences is:*
     Try to be specific, e.g. From my work in a residential home for young people, I learned that I am able to deal with crises calmly and effectively.

   - *My relevant personal or other experiences are:*
     This relates to personal and life experience that you think might be relevant to social work.

   - *What I have learned from these experiences is:*
     Again, try not to generalise and identify specific things that you have learned about yourself or others.

   - *My personal interests/aptitudes are:*
     This could be something like a hobby or skill, or a personal quality that you possess that you think might be helpful for your chosen career of social work.

   - *Key values for me are:*
     Think about what is important to you and why.

   - *I feel I developed these through:*
     Identify specific experiences or people who have been influential in shaping your values.

   - *Skills and knowledge I feel I can offer are:*
     These should be specific to social work.

   - *Skills and knowledge I would like to work on are:*
     Be honest here!

   - *What might stop me/what might I find most difficult?*
     Think about personal issues such as family responsibilities, travelling, access to a computer, etc.

   - *What support might I need?/What strategies might I need to develop?*
     This might be something like a personalised computer or study skills.

3. *Complete the form in as much detail as you can. Then, using the shortcut key combination* (not *the mouse and menu system), select all of the text and reformat it so that all of the text is justified.*
4. *For each section, create a border around the text e.g.*

> My social work (or related) background is:
> Describe any previous social work experience, whether paid or voluntary.
> Before going to study social work, I worked as a health care assistant in a care home for older people.

5. *Using the shortcut key combination, find all instances of the phrase 'social work' and replace with 'social care'. (NB: check carefully that you don't alter other instances of the word 'work'!) How many times do you need to replace it?*
6. *Using the shortcut key combination, delete the title of the form. Rename it 'My Adult Learning Profile'.*
7. *Save in your IT Skills folder and print out a hard copy of your document for your portfolio.*

---

1. *Using Word, create your own Portfolio front sheet using images from ClipArt as well as WordArt. (See Figure 5.5 for an example of how you could do this.) If you have access to the Internet, you will be able to find lots of options for cartoon pictures of computers, etc., but Word itself does contain a number of suitable images.*

2. *Use the outline facility in order to preview how it is going to look before you print it out. This will help to ensure that your creation is balanced aesthetically.*

3. *Save in your IT Skills folder.*

4. *Print out a copy – it doesn't matter if you don't have access to a colour printer, greyscale is fine – and include this as the front sheet for your portfolio.*

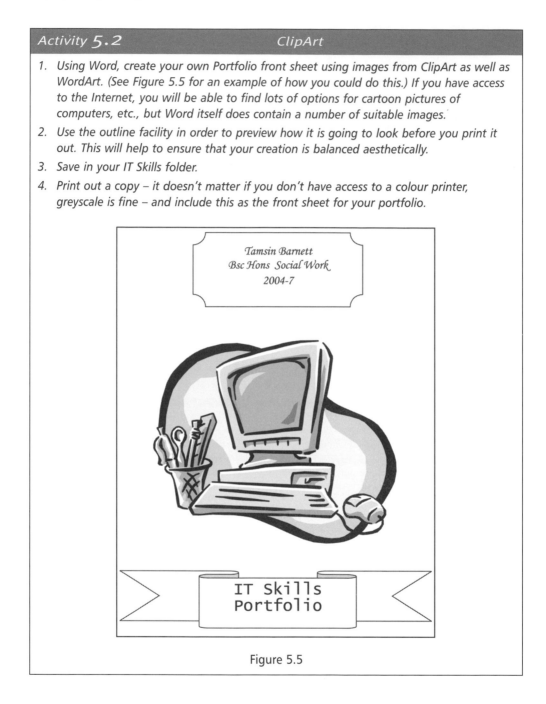

Figure 5.5

Activity 5.3   *Mail merge*

1. *Open up Word and create a new document called 'Carers Group Invite'. Save in your IT Skills folder.*
2. *Create a letterhead for a fictitious social services department or voluntary organisation and type the following template for an invitation letter. Do not include the field names which are contained with the << . . . >>. This document will now be used as the basis for a mail merge.*

Dear <<First name>> <Surname>,

I understand from <<Social worker>> that you are interested in attending a Carers Group that we are starting in the New Year. The first session will be on Tuesday 5th January and subsequent meetings will be on the first Tuesday of every month. We will be meeting in the Acorn Lounge of the Oaktree Centre, off Windlesham Way, from 7.30-9.30pm. We are hoping that the first few sessions will provide an opportunity for you to relax and get to know other carers in an informal environment. Later on, we intend to invite guest speakers according to the expressed wishes of the group.

If you would like to bring <<Name of cared for>> to the first session on 5th Jan, then you are very welcome. However, all sessions after this will be specifically for Carers in order to give you all an opportunity to socialise, share your joys and worries, and above all, have some time and space to be you.

Free transport to and from the group has been negotiated via Hawk Express Taxis and if you would like to take advantage of this, please let <<Social worker>> know by 3rd January.

We look forward to seeing you in the New Year.

Jayne Althrope & Simon Peterson
Social workers

---

3. *Using the basic information below set up the data source listed in Figure 5.6 and save it as 'Potential Group Members'. This will provide the information that will go in the gaps of the letter above.*

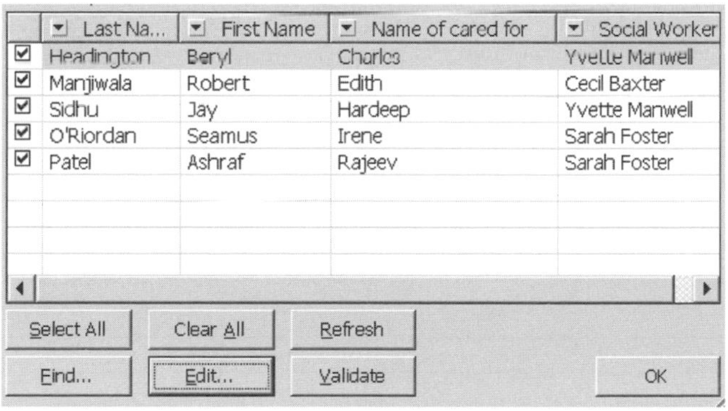

	Last Na...	First Name	Name of cared for	Social Worker
☑	Headington	Beryl	Charles	Yvette Manwell
☑	Manjiwala	Robert	Edith	Cecil Baxter
☑	Sidhu	Jay	Hardeep	Yvette Manwell
☑	O'Riordan	Seamus	Irene	Sarah Foster
☑	Patel	Ashraf	Rajeev	Sarah Foster

Select All   Clear All   Refresh

Find...   Edit...   Validate   OK

Figure 5.6

4. *Merge the data source with the letter and print out a copy of Jay Sidhu's letter.*

Activity 5.4 — Using a template

1. Open up Word and create a curriculum vitae using the template provided. (NB: Word calls a CV a 'résumé'.)

2. Use the Résumé Wizard to create an elegant professional résumé.

3. Include headings of: Professional experience (later rename this as Placements), References, Education, Languages, Volunteer experience and Professional memberships. Also include the heading: Criminal Records Bureau.

4. Fill in all of your personal information. If you do not have anything to put under the heading Professional memberships (e.g. membership of BASW, registered with GSCC), then delete this.

5. Add the heading: Current employer, and supply the relevant information (if a full-time student, write that here).

6. Change the font of the CV to Arial.

7. Save a copy of your completed CV in your IT Skills folder and keep the hard copy to forward to any prospective employers. See the following example.

---

29 FOXTON GARDENS · SHIPLAKE · YORKSHIRE · SH3 8NB
PHONE 0112-231430 · E-MAIL S.BRIDIE1980x@YAHOO.COM

SARAH BRIDIE

EDUCATION & QUALIFICATIONS

1992–1997	Shiplake Secondary School 10 GCSEs grades A*–C
1997–1999	Barking College A-Levels at grades CCD
2003 –	East Acton University College

CURRENT EMPLOYER

Currently a full-time student at East Acton

PLACEMENTS

Year 1   Merton Vale Residential Care Home, Sonnington

This was a 45-day placement in a residential home for Older People with Learning Disabilities

Year 2   Children with Disabilities Team, Acton South

This was a 90-day statutory placement

VOLUNTEER EXPERIENCE

1997–1999   Worked as a Youth Leader with a group run for the siblings of children with disabilities

PROFESSIONAL MEMBERSHIPS

Student member of BASW

LANGUAGES

I am bi-lingual and fluent in English and Spanish

CRIMINAL RECORDS BUREAU

At the beginning of my degree course, I was CRB checked by the university and have current full clearance

REFERENCES

To be supplied on request

Activity 5.5   Spell checker

1. *Create a new document in Word entitled 'A Harsh Form of Justice'.*
2. *Copy type the article reproduced below. Don't worry about correcting any typing errors or spelling mistakes you make.*
3. *Change the font of the article to Verdana and double-space all of the lines. Make sure that the margins are justified so that they appear as below.*
4. *Now check for any typos or spelling mistakes. Correct these using the spell checker.*
5. *Save and print out the corrected article with a footer indicating where it has been saved and the number of pages and place in your IT Skills portfolio.*

A Harsh Form of Justice

Anti-social behaviour orders (ASBOs) were introduced in 1999. Since then, there has been no clear definition of anti-social behaviour, nor any evidence to suggest that the orders have a positive effect on the rates of re-offending. Nevertheless, government support for this method of punishing offenders was shown in October 2004 when Lord Falconer announced that the courts were to be given more powers to impose ASBOs and that a witness protection scheme was to be introduced for more vulnerable witnesses.

Already the number of orders has increased. Only 785 orders were issued in the first three years, but since November 2003 more than 2,600 have been issued. This huge increase in numbers is being challenged not only by probation officers but also by those who see that offensive behaviour often derives from mental illness, drug addiction or alcoholism which the ASBO does not address. And so an alliance made up of charities, professionals, trade unions, community groups, young people and others is urging the government to carry out a full public review of the orders and the way they are used.

Breaches result in excessive penalties

While anti-social behaviour causes distress and misery, the current response is not just, appropriate or effective. Questions about justice arise firstly from the fact that orders made in a civil court, if breached, can result in penalties far higher for the same misdemeanour than would apply in a criminal action. Secondly, injustices can result from the way the system is administered. Applications for orders are made by the police or the local authority to the magistrates court which acts in a civil capacity. The magistrate grants the order on the balance of probabilities, issuing a civil order which requires a lower standard of proof than that required in a criminal action. Professional witnesses or councillors can give evidence on behalf of victims, who are not required to be in court. Breach of the order, even if the offence would not be sufficient to justify a prison sentence were it tried in the criminal court, can result in imprisonment for anything up to five years. In making the order, furthermore, magistrates are empowered to add additional constraints to those requested by the applicant and a breach of any of these additional restrictions may also be heavily penalised.

The Napo review puts this into perspective. A 26-year-old homeless beggar banned from begging breached the order and was given 24 months' custody. After eight months he was discharged, offended again and was awarded three years in jail. His solicitor pointed out that the 26-year-old received five years' imprisonment for an offence which under criminal law would not warrant imprisonment.

Similarly a profoundly deaf girl was served with an order for spitting in public, and having broken it was committed to prison on remand. In both these situations reasonable observers might see an injustice; not only because the ASBO results in a punishment for an offence which English law does not usually regard as sufficient to justify imprisonment, but also because the perpetrators seem less like villains than vulnerable individuals needing guidance. Because the ASBO does nothing to sort out the reasons for the offensive behaviour, since November 2003 almost 50% of orders have been breached. In 2001, 114 of 322 ASBOs ended in the offender being jailed, and in 2002, 212 of 403 orders were breached and the offenders went to prison.

Injustice may also occur where the authority is short-staffed and work is hurried. An order requires a letter to the offender, a home visit, a warning letter and an acceptable behaviour contract. Fast-tracking may play a part in the huge increase in the number of orders served. Offenders may be sent to prison because all of the restrictions in the order have not been understood. In Manchester a youth appeared in court for breaching his ASBO, the order having been made in his absence without the youth having the chance to give his side of the story. The day after, when someone came to his house to 'serve' him the order, he was handed a bulky document of several dozen pages with no explanation or attempt to ascertain whether he was able to understand its contents. Because he had not read parts of the document he breached three times the restriction barring him from a certain estate and associating with certain others. Now he may be sent to prison.

The expansion of ASBOs

Originally, ASBOs were meant to be used only for offences that could not be dealt with effectively by other legislation. Extensions of the law have broadened their use with no assurance that they are the most appropriate response to a situation. In some instances young people could indeed have been dealt with under childcare legislation. Indeed, the panel meetings at which the orders are discussed seem similar to local authority case conferences or reviews, and the panel members' responsibility is to balance their concern for the welfare of people living in the area with the future welfare of the offender.

The offender might not be present to make his own case and usually has no support from friends or parents who might act as advocates. It would be more appropriate for ASBOs to be attached to some sort of statutory supervision. Why are these young people being denied their rights to receive care under childcare legislation?

If ASBOs are intended to divert people from crime, we have no real evidence that this is being achieved. Overall, the numbers in prison are increasing rather than decreasing, children are being named and shamed in local papers, and the publicity given to their misbehaviour has made it more difficult for them to resettle and obtain work after time in prison. BASW members may want to support ASBO concerns in its request for the government to review the effectiveness of orders which might result in whole families being evicted. In an inclusive society we need to have properly funded community and youth service with support for people with mental health, drug, alcohol and other social problems.

(Source: McLeod V (2005) A harsh form of justice, Professional Social Work, May, 16–17)

Activity 5.6   *Inserting pictorial characters/symbols*

1. *Devise a simple poster inviting the reader to attend an activity that you might organise.*
2. *Include a number of different symbols or pictorial characters to illustrate it – do not include those from ClipArt! (See the example in Figure 5.7.)*
3. *Save in your IT Skills folder.*

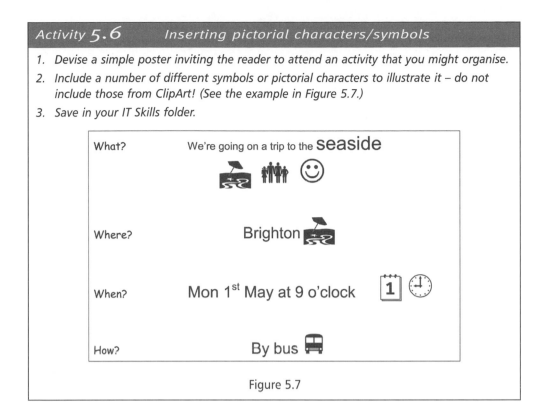

Figure 5.7

Activity 5.7   *Creating/inserting a table*

1. Create a table using the following one as a template. This will then be used as a checklist for you to ensure that you are on track for completing all of the activities. There are 50 different activities in this book, so make sure that you include a row for each one.
2. Apply a border and 'Style' format to the table as in the example provided here.

Activity Name	Software Package	Date
1		
2		
3		
4		
5		
6		
7		
8		
9		
10		
11		
12		
13		
14		
15		
16		
17		
18		
19		
20		

3. Print off a copy and insert your completed table after your front sheet (Activity 5.2). Make sure that you tick off Activity 5.7.
4. Save in your IT Skills Folder using an appropriate file name.

Activity 5.8 — Inserting an organisation chart

1. Open up a blank Word document.
2. Create an organisation chart demonstrating the lines of authority/accountability in any social care agency that you are familiar with. Alternatively, create an organisation chart demonstrating the way that social work is organised in another country.
3. Save to your IT Skills folder and print off a copy. Figure 5.8 is an example of how a university is structured.

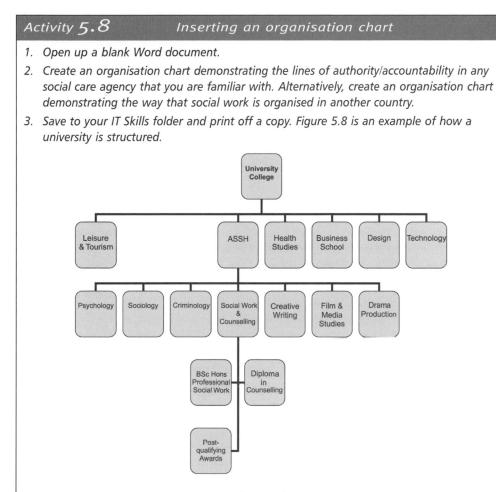

Figure 5.8

Chapter 6
Spreadsheets

Spreadsheets are used across social care organisations in order to organise and present statistical information, such as numbers and types of client contacts in order to justify and plan for future service provision. Spreadsheets are not only used for statistical data requiring the use of formulas, but also for non-numerical data such as contact details. Whilst social workers may not necessarily need to create a spreadsheet themselves, they need to be able to open up basic spreadsheets and add information or extract information from them. For example, contact details for potential foster carers may be contained on a departmental spreadsheet. The supervising social worker may need to update essential information without feeling intimidated by the software. Some service users may have complex financial situations that require exploring and managing and therefore a simple spreadsheet may be able to assist with budgeting.

Spreadsheets can also generate graphs and charts, which are often far more effective in assisting people with numeracy difficulties to make sense of confusing figures. Graphs and charts can also enhance the visual presentation of any research that you may undertake in the course of your social work studies.

Getting started

For the purposes of the ECDL you will need to familiarise yourself with Microsoft Excel, although there are many other commercial spreadsheet software packages available such as Lotus 1-2-3 or CalcStar. In order to access Excel from the desktop you need to select it from 'Programs' on the Start Menu or click on the icon shown in Figure 6.1.

Figure 6.1

You will then be taken to a blank spreadsheet which represents a bookkeeping ledger with columns and rows waiting to be filled with numerical or textual data. Each box on a spreadsheet is known as a 'cell' and has its own unique identifying address or cell reference. A spreadsheet may be made up of more than one 'sheet' and you can move between them by clicking on the tab-like buttons at the bottom of the screen.

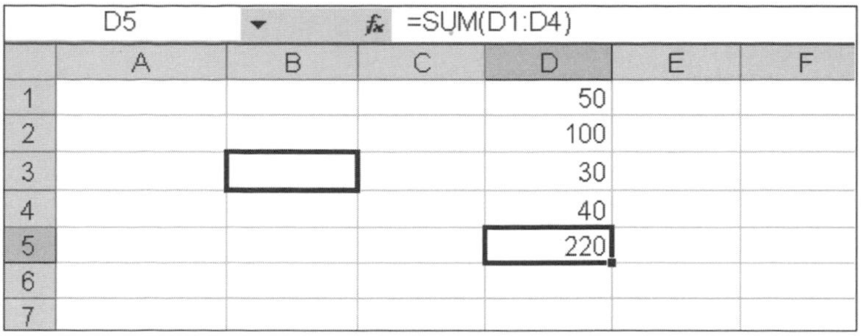

D5	▼	*fx* =SUM(D1:D4)			
A	**B**	**C**	**D**	**E**	**F**
1			50		
2			100		
3			30		
4			40		
5			220		
6					
7					

Figure 6.2

In Figure 6.2, the address of the number 220 in the highlighted cell is **D5** and this address appears in the 'address bar' in the top left of the screen. The address of the other highlighted cell is **B3.**

You can enter either text or numbers into the cells, and the spreadsheet package is able to perform complex calculations on figures entered without needing the additional services of a calculator. If you look at all of the cells in column D above you will note that the figures in D1–D4 have been added together in order to give the 'sum' of 220. This calculation was performed with the assistance of a 'formula' which appears in the 'formula bar' next to the 'address bar'. Formulae can be used to add, subtract, multiply, find the average, count and carry out many other mathematical functions and all have a basic format similar to the one above. By double-clicking on the **fx** button, a pop-up menu appears and you can select the relevant formula or function.

Spreadsheets use the following symbols for mathematical calculations:

- * for multiplication
- / for division
- + for addition
- − for subtraction

It is important to remember that if you are asking the spreadsheet to perform complex calculations that involve more than one calculation, then the order above will be applied. Therefore, 10*5+6 will give the answer 56, not 110. If you want to achieve the latter result you would need to write the formula as 10*(5+6) as the spreadsheet will work out the calculation in brackets first.

As with Word, the main features of Excel can be accessed via shortcuts on the toolbar, or via pull-down menus from the top of the screen. You can save and open existing spreadsheets from the 'File' menu and this menu also allows you to print out a specific highlighted area of the spreadsheet. This is an invaluable function as it means that when you are working with large amounts of data, you do not have to print out the entire spreadsheet.

The 'Insert' menu allows you to insert extra rows, columns and cells after you have started working on your spreadsheet. It also allows you to open the Chart Wizard and enter a chart or graph directly into your spreadsheet. However, you are probably more likely to click on the Chart icon on the toolbar if wishing to create any chart or graph.

The 'Format' pull-down menu is helpful for altering the visual presentation of your spreadsheet and allows you to change the font size and add colours and borders to cells. This formatting can be applied to individual cells or the entire spreadsheet and is retained even when the spreadsheet is pasted into another file such as a Word document. This menu also allows you to format how numbers will be displayed in cells, e.g. with a '£' sign, as a percentage, or as a fraction.

One of the most useful shortcut icons on the toolbar when working with text data is the one shown in Figure 6.3.

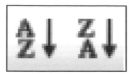

Figure 6.3

This allows for the alphabetical ordering of text that appears in the same column e.g. if you have entered surnames of individuals into column A randomly and would like them to be alphabetically ordered you can click on this icon. Not only will the column containing the surnames be ordered alphabetically, but, provided that the rest of the sheet is highlighted, any other data relating to that individual will also be re-ordered in order to ensure that all records still match.

Have a go now at Activities 6.1–6.8 that cover the basic aspects of Excel.

Activity *6.1* *Creating a spreadsheet*

1. *Create a table in Excel using the following data. In column A, include the categories below, missing out the first cell and beginning with row 2:*

- *Population (thousands) under age 18 in 2003*
- *Population (thousands) under age 5 in 2003*
- *Population annual growth rate 1970–1990 (%)*
- *Population annual growth rate 1990–2003 (%)*
- *Crude death rate in 1970*
- *Crude death rate in 2003*
- *Crude birth rate in 1970*
- *Crude birth rate in 2003*
- *Life expectancy in 1970*
- *Life expectancy in 2003*
- *Total fertility rate in 2003*
- *% population urbanised in 2003*
- *Average annual growth rate of urban population 1970–1990 (%)*
- *Average annual growth rate of urban population 1990–2003 (%)*
- *No. of phone sets per 100 people in 2002*
- *No. of Internet users per 100 people in 2002*

2. *Now create further columns B–H with the headings of the countries below and include the following data.*

Brazil	Iran	Italy	South Africa	UK	Zimbabwe	USA
60357	27281	9779	17770	13275	6557	75893
16663	6205	2573	4778	3352	1890	20794
2.2	3.4	0.3	2.4	0.2	3.5	1
1.4	1.5	0.1	1.5	0.3	1.6	1.1
11	14	10	14	12	13	9
7	5	11	18	10	28	8
35	43	17	38	16	49	17
20	21	9	22	11	32	15
59	54	72	53	72	55	71
68	70	79	47	78	33	77
2.2	2.3	1.2	2.6	1.6	3.9	2.1
83	67	67	57	89	35	80
3.6	4.9	0.4	2.5	0.9	6.1	1.1
2.2	2.8	0.2	2.7	0.4	3	1.6
42	22	142	41	143	6	113
8	5	35	7	42	4	55

3. *Ensure that all columns are wide enough in order to display the full name of each country. Add this title to the spreadsheet:*

   Source: **www.unicef.org/infobycountry/index.html** *accessed 18/7/05*
4. *Save the table as 'Unicef Demographic Comparisions' in your IT Skills folder.*
5. *Copy the table to either Word or PowerPoint. Save the copied table in its new application as a separate document in your IT Skills folder and include a printout in your portfolio.*

Example:

	No of Phone sets per 100 People in 2002	Brazil	Iran	Italy	South Africa	UK
Population (thousands) under age 18 in 2003		60357	27281	9779	17770	13275
Population (thousands) under age 5 in 2003		16663	6205	2573	4778	3352
Population Annual Growth Rate 1970–1990 (%)	People in 2002	2.2	3.4	0.3	2.4	0.2
Population Annual Growth Rate 1990–2003 (%)		1.4	1.5	0.1	1.5	0.3
Crude Death Rate in 1970	No of Internet	11	14	10	14	12
Crude Death Rate in 2003		7	5	11	18	10
Crude Birth Rate in 1970	Users per 100	35	43	17	38	16
Crude Birth Rate in 2003	People	20	21	9	22	11
Life Expectancy in 1970	in 2002	59	54	72	53	72
Life Expectancy in 2003		68	70	79	47	78
Total Fertility Rate in 2003		2.2	2.3	1.2	2.6	1.6
% Population Urbanised in 2003		83	67	67	57	89
Average Annual Growth Rate of the Urban Population 1970–1990 (%)		3.6	4.9	0.4	2.5	0.9
Average Annual Growth Rate of Urban Population 1990–2003 (%)		2.2	2.8	0.2	2.7	0.4
		42	22	142	143	143
		8	5	35	7	42

Source: **www.unicef.org/infobycountry/index.html** *Accessed 18/7/05*

Activity 6.2   *Reading and printing out an existing spreadsheet*

1. Open the Excel spreadsheet 'Unicef Demographic Comparisons' that you created in the previous activity.
2. In the spreadsheet's current format you should be able to see the full details of all of the countries. Hide the columns containing the data for Italy and the USA, but leave the other countries' data on view.
3. Go to the web address given in Activity 6.1 and locate two more countries along with their data to add in two new columns to the spreadsheet. (You will need to find the 'Statistics' section of the country's webpage.) Add the data in the relevant rows.
4. Once you have done this, set up the printing options so that you print the amended spreadsheet (i.e. minus Italy and the USA, but including your two new countries) and only print up to Row 12 (i.e. Total Fertility Rate in 2003).
5. Print out the page in landscape view and include in your portfolio. Save the amended spreadsheet in your IT Skills folder.

Activity 6.3   *Formatting a spreadsheet*

1. Open up the original spreadsheet 'Unicef Demographic Comparisons'.
2. Re-format the spreadsheet in the following ways:

   a. Select a different font for all headings.
   b. Change the font for the figures.
   c. Change the background colour for the first row containing the names of the countries.
   d. Change the background colour for the first column containing the data categories.
   e. Insert dashed gridlines to separate the columns. Create a border around the table.

3. Save the amended spreadsheet as a separate file in your IT Skills folder and print off a copy for your portfolio (don't worry if you don't have a colour printer).

Activity 6.4   *Creating pie/column charts*

1. Using the information below taken from the 2001 Census relating to the postal district HP11 2JZ, enter the figures into an Excel spreadsheet.
2. Create a pie chart of the overall Wycombe population describing their health (NB: the example in Figure 6.4 refers to the Wycombe 015b population).
3. Create a column chart of all of the statistics contained within the table.
4. Save the spreadsheet in your IT Skills folder and copy your two charts into a Word document with your name at the top. Print the document.

The 2001 Census asked people to describe their health over the preceding 12 months as 'good', 'fairly good' or 'not good'. People were also asked if they had any limiting long-term illness, health problem or disability that restricted their daily activities or the work they could do.

The 2001 Census asked a question about any voluntary care provided to look after, or give any help or support to family members, friends, neighbours or others because of long-term physical or mental ill-health or disability, or problems relating to old age. In the Wycombe sub-area (015b) 5.6 per cent of the resident population provided unpaid care compared to 10 per cent in England and Wales. Of the people providing unpaid care, 27.7 per cent gave 50 hours or more per week, this compared with 20.9 per cent in England and Wales.

	Wycombe 015B	Abbey	Wycombe	South East	England and Wales
General health: Good	71.03	75.37	74.45	71.50	68.55
General health: Fairly good	21.50	18.99	19.64	21.38	22.23
General health: Not good	7.46	5.64	5.91	7.12	9.22
People with a limiting long-term illness	13.74	11.46	12.63	15.47	18.23
People of working age with a limiting long-term illness	7.55	7.24	8.39	10.63	13.56
Households with one or more person with a limiting long-term illness	24.60	25.64	26.07	29.36	34.05

Percentage of resident population in each group, April 2001

Source: **neighbourhood.statistics.gov.uk/dissemination/AreaProfile1.do?tab=3**
Accessed 12/5/05

See examples in Figures 6.4 and 6.5

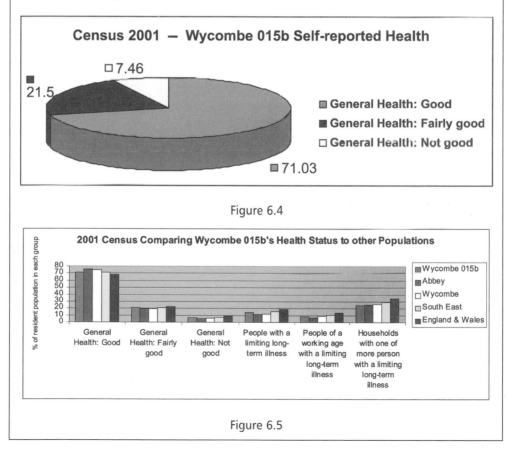

Figure 6.4

Figure 6.5

Activity 6.5 — Ordering data alphabetically

1. Create a new spreadsheet entitled 'Benefit Rates' and enter in the following headers:

Name of Benefit	Amount Payable	Age Entitlement	
		Minimum Age	Maximum Age
Disability Living Allowance: Care: Middle rate			
Maternity Allowance			
Job Seekers Allowance			
Industrial Injuries Benefit			
Disability Living Allowance: Care: Higher rate			
Incapacity Benefit			
Guardians Allowance			
Paternity Allowance			
Disability Living Allowance: Mobility: Higher rate			
Child Benefit			
Disability Living Allowance: Care: Lower rate			
Attendance Allowance			
Carers Allowance			
Income Support			
Severe Disability Allowance			
Disability Living Allowance: Mobility: Lower rate			

2. Fill in the relevant figures – you may need to search the web to find up-to-date rates. Don't worry if some of the benefits have multiple categories (e.g. Income support is paid at different rates according to age or whether part of a couple), just select one rate to input.

3. Order the names of the benefits alphabetically. Make sure that they still match the relevant benefit figure.

4. Order the benefits further by minimum age – e.g. bracket together all of the benefits that are payable from birth up to 16/65/+.

5. Save in your IT Skills folder.

Activity 6.6   Using the SUM formula

1. Create a new spreadsheet entitled 'Income/Expenditure' to assist a client (or yourself) with managing debt repayments over the forthcoming year.

2. In the first column, create cells under the following income categories:
   a. Wages
   b. State benefits
   c. Maintenance
   d. Rent (received from lodger)
   e. Other
   f. TOTAL

3. Leave two columns' gap and then create cells under the following expenditure categories:
   a. Rent/mortgage
   b. Electricity
   c. Gas
   d. Water
   e. Council Tax
   f. Food
   g. Clothes
   h. Transport
   i. Insurance
   j. Childcare
   k. Going out
   l. Cigarettes
   m. Other
   n. TOTAL

4. Leave two columns' gap and then create cells under the following outstanding debts categories:
   a. Priority debts (e.g. rent/Council Tax)
   b. Non-priority debts (e.g. credit cards)
   c. TOTAL
   d. TOTAL amount left from income to pay off debts

5. Now enter figures into each of these categories, based either on yourself or a known or fictitious client. Make sure that they are all either weekly or monthly, otherwise your sums will not make sense.

6. Once you have entered all of the figures, you will need to create a sum formula in order to add up all of the figures. Create a sum formula in the TOTAL cells for each category.

7. Now you will need to work out how much money you have remaining out of the income once all of the expenditures have been accounted for. Therefore create a subtraction formula for the total of income minus the total of expenditure in the cell you created for 4d (see above).

8. *If you have a negative figure (highly likely!) try tweaking some of the figures in the expenditure column in order to balance the sheet. Even if your figures do balance, try changing them to ensure that your SUM formula works.*

9. *Save the spreadsheet to your IT Skills folder.*

Example:

Your spreadsheet should be similar (but with figures included) to the one below.

<u>Income/Expenditure Spreadsheet for Debt Management</u>

Income		Expenditure		Debts	
Wages		Rent/mortgage		Priority Debts	
State Benefits		Electricity		Non-priority Debts	
Maintenance		Gas		TOTAL	
Rent (received from lodger)		Water			
Other		Council Tax			
		Food			
		Clothes			
		Transport			
		Insurance			
		Childcare			
		Going out			
		Cigarettes			
		Other			
TOTAL		*TOTAL*		*TOTAL amount left*	

Activity 6.7   *Creating and moving between data sheets*

1. *Open up Excel. Create a new spreadsheet titled 'Attendance at Parenting Group'.*
2. *Create separate worksheets for each month of the year, as in Figure 6.6.*

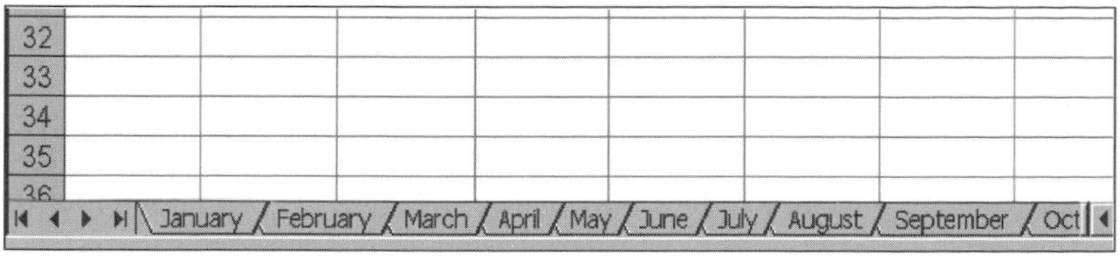

Figure 6.6.

3. *In the January sheet create a list of at least ten fictitious clients who have been invited to attend the Parenting Group.*
4. *Copy this list of clients across to each of the subsequent months.*
5. *Insert a row at the top of each sheet and type in the dates of each session. You should therefore end up with four columns per client per month.*
6. *Create some fictitious data about the clients' attendance, i.e. put either 'Yes' or 'No' for each client against each date on each sheet, as in the following example:*

Client Name	Date of Session			
	03/01/2005	10/01/2005	17/01/2005	25/01/2005
Jayne Tomlins	Yes	Yes	Yes	Yes
Frank Tomlins	No	No	Yes	No
Serena Fachey	Yes	Yes	Yes	Yes
Tracey Dodd	Yes	No	No	No
Amity Jacobs	Yes	Yes	Yes	Yes
George Jacobs	No	Yes	Yes	Yes
Christine O'Donohue	Yes	No	Yes	Yes
Simone Tyree	No	Yes	Yes	Yes
Jamie Hathaway	Yes	Yes	Yes	Yes
Fariah Constantine	Yes	Yes	Yes	Yes
Precious Oleywole	Yes	Yes	Yes	Yes
Amy Lovelace	No	No	No	No
Zoe Prestwick	Yes	Yes	No	Yes

7. *Alter the format for the header columns on your January worksheet and format all of the client names so that they are italicised.*
8. *Copy this formatting across to all of the other month worksheets.*
9. *Save your Spreadsheet in your IT Skills folder and print out the worksheet for March.*

Activity 6.8	Using the COUNTIF formula

1. *Open up your 'Attendance at Parenting Group' spreadsheet. Start working on the January worksheet.*

2. *Create a new column titled 'Total Attendance'. In this column use the COUNTIF formula to add up the total amount of times that each individual parent has attended. (NB: COUNTIF is a formula that is able to count text within a spreadsheet and therefore will be able to count the number of times that 'Yes' has been entered in the spreadsheet.)*

3. *Once you have totals for each parent's attendance in January, copy the COUNTIF formula across to the following worksheets up to and including June so that the spreadsheet calculates monthly totals for each parent. You should then have six totals.*

4. *Return to January's worksheet and create another new column entitled 'Total Attendance over duration of Group'.*

5. *Create a SUM formula to calculate in this column the total amount of times that each individual parent has attended the group in the period January–June. You will need to include the totals from each monthly worksheet. See the following table for an example of how your completed January worksheet should look.*

6. *Save your completed Spreadsheet as 'Total Attendance at Parenting Group' in your IT Skills folder and print out January's worksheet.*

Example

Client Name	Date of Session				Total Attendance in January	Total Attendance over Course of Group
	03/01/2005	10/01/2005	17/01/2005	25/01/2005		
Jayne Tomlins	Yes	Yes	Yes	Yes	4	4
Frank Tomlins	No	No	Yes	No	1	6
Serena Fachey	Yes	Yes	Yes	Yes	4	24
Tracey Dodd	Yes	No	No	No	1	6
Amity Jacobs	Yes	Yes	Yes	Yes	4	24
George Jacobs	No	Yes	Yes	Yes	3	14
Christine O'Donohue	Yes	No	Yes	Yes	3	18
Simone Tyree	No	Yes	Yes	Yes	3	18
Jamie Hathaway	Yes	Yes	Yes	Yes	4	24
Fariah Constantine	Yes	Yes	Yes	Yes	4	24
Precious Oleywole	Yes	Yes	Yes	Yes	4	24
Amy Lovelace	No	No	No	No	0	0
Zoe Prestwick	Yes	Yes	No	Yes	3	18

Chapter 7
Databases

Most local authorities have now bought into complex database systems that allow users at multiple levels to access and alter information relating to service users. At the most basic level, the customer database can be used to search to see if an individual or family is known to social care. This level of searching and inputting may be done by customer service officers or social work assistants. The next level up is that required of social workers involving adding and altering case records relating to service users, including adding detailed and confidential information relating to their interventions. This information can then be manipulated in order to produce care plans, assessments and other reports. Some social workers may also be required to enter financial assessments into the database. Examples of databases that you may use in local authorities include CRIS, SWIFT and CareFirst.

In addition to databases used by local authorities, you may also need to access academic databases in order to carry out research for essays or your dissertation. These databases contain references to thousands of journal articles and books relating to social care and are invaluable resources when exploring a topic in depth. Some of these databases, such as ASSIA, may require the use of an ATHENS password (usually available from your library helpdesk); others such as SCIE's Social Care Online are freely available on the Internet.

This chapter explores using pre-built databases as well as outlining the basic principles behind building your own using a database software package.

Getting started

Although you are more likely to utilise a pre-built database during the course of your work as a social worker, the ECDL requires competence in Microsoft Access which allows you to create databases as well as utilising pre-constructed ones. Access can be opened via the icon shown in Figure 7.1.

Figure 7.1

Microsoft Access is able to create what is known as a 'relational database'. This means that not only is the database able to hold basic information or records (like a card index system) but it can also relate different collections of information (e.g. multiple card index systems) provided that they have fields in common. For example, an Access database could contain tables of information about children registered on the Child Protection Register:

| Personal Information | Parental Details | School Details | Registration Criteria |

All of the tables would contain the name of the child (which would be known as the 'key field') and this would enable all of the tables to be linked together within one database.

Unlike the other software applications already covered you do not get automatically directed into a blank template from which you can start working. You will either have to select a pre-existing database to work from, or you will be asked to create a new database by initially selecting where and by what name you wish to save it.

Figure 7.2

After clicking on 'Create' the box shown in Figure 7.2 will then appear in the middle of the screen. For basic database use you will need to familiarise yourself with the following database functions or 'objects' that can be found on the left-hand size of this box:

- Tables
- Queries
- Forms
- Reports

'Tables' are where all of the information in your database is stored and until you have created one, none of the other functions can work. The table looks a bit like a spreadsheet. Simple databases only have one table and in order to help you gain confidence in using Access, Activities 7.1, 7.2 and 7.3 only use one table. You can navigate your way around the table in a variety of different ways: using the tab key, the cursor keys, clicking on the record that you require or by using the navigation buttons on the bottom left of the screen:

Figure 7.3

'Queries' are basically searches that you carry out on your information. For example, you may wish to carry out a query on how many children aged 11 are on the Child Protection Register. However, if you simply wish to find one specific record within a table, you could use the shortcut 'Find' function Ctrl + F or the binoculars icon on the toolbar. The relevant record would then be highlighted.

'Forms' are very similar to the tables, but they can be designed to be more user-friendly when you come to inputting records.

Finally, 'Reports' are used to print out information from the database. Rather than having to print out the entire database, you can create a report that will generate only records created by a specific query.

Whilst Access can be a bit confusing to navigate, it does have helpful Wizards for each of the above 'objects' to assist you in building your database. If you don't want to use the Wizard to help you build your database then you can go to the 'Design View' of the database which is essentially the behind-the-scenes part and slightly less user-friendly as in parts it requires some coding.

Have a go now at Activities 7.1–7.8 to practise your database building and searching skills.

Activity 7.1	Creating a database using Access

1. Open up Access and create a database file 'Client Contact Details'. Make sure that this is saved in your IT Skills folder.

2. Design a table in design view using the following information:

Field Name	Data Type
Client name	Text
Key worker	Text
Organisation	Text
Tel no	Memo
Address	Text
E-mail address	Hyperlink

3. Save the table as 'Key Worker Contact Details'. (Don't worry about creating a primary key if a pop-up box asks you.)

4. Now add the following records to this table:

*   Jasmin Freeman; Jack Wainwright; Canterbury Carers; 01765-44312; 23a Chaucer Court, Canterbury; jack@cantcare.org.uk

*   Benjamin Sutherland; Pedro Garcia; Help the Aged; 01765-45861; Beech House, 223 London Rd, Canterbury; p.garcia@helptheaged.co.uk

*   Lorenzo Gonzales; Sally Matthews; District Nurse; 01765-42212; Haleacre Surgery, Mere Close, Canterbury; sally.matthews@canterbury.nhs.gov.uk

*   Cathy Clarke; Jackie Smith; District Nurse; 01765-42212; Haleacre Surgery, Mere Close, Canterbury; Jackie.smith@canterbury.nhs.gov.uk

*   Jay Hardeep; Paul Vickers; Fastnet Home Alarms; 08456-33333; Fastnet House, Buxton Business Park, Eastleigh; pvickers@fastnet.com

*   Amy Boden; Mark van der Tweel; Chaucer Day Centre; 01765-43126; East Street, Canterbury; m.vandertweel@kent.gov.uk

*   Chris Speake; Patience Ojeama; Reliance Homecare; 01765-488943; 12 Meridian Way, Canterbury; patience@reliance.cant.uk

*   Rajeev Patel; Brenda Fothergill; FSG Homecare; 01765-422990; 3 Gants Court, Acacia Avenue, Canterbury; brenda1@fsg.org.uk

5. Order your records alphabetically by organisation name.

6. Save the table and print out all of your records in landscape format ensuring that the full details are visible for each field (you don't need to create a report to do this.)

Activity 7.2   *Opening an existing database using Access*

1. Open up the Access file 'Client Contact Details' as created in the previous activity.
2. Set the Primary Key as the 'Client Name' field.
3. Using the Form Wizard, create a form in order to enter some new records into your table. You will need to include all of the fields that you have already created in the table. Add four new records using the form with two of the records involving workers who are connected to the Chaucer Day Centre. Make sure that you save the additional records.
4. Sort the records so that they appear alphabetically by client name.
5. Staying within the Form view, filter the records so that you are only able to see the records that relate to workers connected with Chaucer Day Centre. You should be able to view just three records now if you scroll through the form.
6. Stay in the Form view and print out all twelve records. (You do not need to create a report to do this.)

Activity 7.3   *Exporting an existing database to Excel*

1. Open up the database 'Client Contact Details' that you have just been working on.
2. Open up the table 'Key Worker Contact Details'. Export the file to Excel and save as an Excel file in your IT Skills folder.
3. Open Excel and view your data ensuring that all of the columns are wide enough for you to see it all. Save.
4. Print out a copy of your newly created spreadsheet in landscape format in Excel.

Activity 7.4	*Creating a relational database using Access*

1. Open up the database 'Contact Details'. You should have one form and one table saved under the title 'Key Worker Contact Details'. You now need to create another table called 'Client Contact Details'.

2. Create the following fields for this new table:

Field Name	Data Type
Client name	Text
Tel no	Memo
Address	Text
Client group	Text

3. Make sure that you set the Primary Key to the 'Client name' field.

4. Now enter in details for the clients created in the previous activity. You can use the same 'Client group' – community care – for all of the clients, but need to create fictitious contact details.

5. You now need to create another table called 'Family Contact Details'. Create the following fields for this new table:

field Name	Data Type
Contact name	Text
Relationship	Text
Tel no	Memo
Address	Text
Client name	Text

6. Enter in details for ten individuals who must be linked to clients created in the previous table via the Client name (which again should be your Primary Key).

7. Go to the Relationships view and create relationships between the tables using the Primary Key. Print a copy of the relationships once you have done this. You are ready to start searching your database.

Activity 7.5   *Carrying out a search in Access*

1. Open up Access and your database 'Client Contact Details'.
2. Create a simple query to search the database purely on the following fields:
   - Client name
   - Key worker
   - Contact name
   - Tel no.
3. Save this query as 'Simple Query'.
4. Now create a more complex query to produce information on clients connected to the Chaucer Day Centre. Include all available fields, but limit the search to the Chaucer Day Centre clients. Save as 'Complex Query'.
5. Create a printout of the records relating to this query (you don't need to create a report for this).

Activity 7.6   *Creating a report using Access*

1. Open Access and your 'Client Contact Details' database.
2. Using the complex query that you generated in the previous activity, create a report to print out the three records that matched the query criteria.
3. Use the following formatting styles:
   - Aligned left
   - Landscape
   - Casual
4. Rename the report so that the title appears as 'Chaucer Day Centre Users'.
5. Create a printout of your report.

Activity 7.7   *Using the agency database*

When working for a local authority, or in a statutory setting, you will be required to familiarise yourself with your agency's recording and database system. This may involve being sent on a training course. By the end of the placement, you should be able to both enter and retrieve basic information from the system.

Print out a client record sheet from a local authority database, e.g. SWIFT, CRIS or CareFirst. This should be suitably anonymised but ideally should contain your user ID to demonstrate that you accessed the information. See Figure 7.4 for an example.

Core Information Initial CONTACT & Risk ASSESSMENT		Printed Date: 26-JUL-2005

Initial Contact Information		

Individual Client Patient Details (S + R)

NHS Number: 1235465765	Social Care ID (Swift): 315832	National Insurance Number: TP10242A

Title: Mr	Surname: Test	First Name: Mobile	Other Names:

Home Address:
Chesham Bois Manor Amersham Road , Chesham, Buckinghamshire

County: Buckinghamshire	Postcode: HP5 1NE

Tel: (Home) 01494 534712	Tel: (Work)	Tel: (Mobile)

Address if different from home address:

County:	Postcode:

Tel: (of different address)

DOB: 13-OCT-1903	Gender: Male	Marital Status: Widowed

Lives alone: Yes X No	Language /Communication used: English

Race/Ethnic Origin: White British	Nationality: British	Religion: Christian

Hearing Impairment Yes X No	Interpreter/Assistance required: Y
Speech Impairment Yes X No	
Visual Impairment Yes X No	

Information Provided to the Assessor by:

Name: R Aitchison	Relationship: Primary Health

Address:
Wycombe General Hospital Queen Alexandra Road , High Wycombe, Buckinghamshire

County: Buckinghamshire	Postcode: HP11 2TT

Tel No: (01494) 526161

Method of Contact: Telephone	Is the client aware of the referrral: Yes No X

Name:	Relationship: Primary Health

Address:

County:	Postcode:

Tel No:

Letter	Is the client aware of the referrral: Yes No X

Hospital Discharge (section 2 Notification)

Name of Hospital: Wycombe General	Name of Hospital Consultant: Dr Smith

Ward Name/Number: 5a	Ward Type:	Ward Tel No:

Emergency Admission	Yes	No	Date of Admission: 25 7 05
Planned Admission	Yes	No X	Expected Discharge Date: 29 7 05
Compulsory Admission	Yes	No	Actual Discharge Date:

Likely Length of Stay: 7 days

Reason for referral to social care:
Admitted to hospital, Broken neck of femur.

Has the patient consented to referral to Social Care?	Yes X	No

Date of Contact made from ward: 26 7 05	Time Contact made from ward:

Date Contact Form* received from acute services: 26 7 05	Time Contact Form* received from acute services:

*Further Assessments to commence within 3 days of receipt of this Contact Assessment.

Figure 7.4

Activity 7.8 *Using a research database*

1. Log on to SCIE's social work database **www.scie-socialcareonline.org.uk/**. *This database is regularly updated and contains references to journal articles and books published internationally on issues relating to social work. It is therefore an invaluable tool to utilise when writing academic assignments or undertaking a literature review for your dissertation.*

2. *Carry out a 'Simple Search' on the topic of transracial adoption.*

3. *Sort the records by publication date.*

4. *Select six records of interest to you. These could be journal articles, websites or books. Once you have highlighted six records, view them in full (at the moment you will only be able to see a brief description of the entry).*

5. *Print out your six selected records for your portfolio.*

6. *Carry out some more complex searches now: How many entries does the database retrieve for:*

   a. *articles written by June Thoburn on the subject of adoption?*

   b. *articles written about adoption and permanency planning?*

   c. *books written by Diana Hinings published by Penguin?*

   d. *articles written by David Howe in 2001?*

7. *Imagine that you have been given this as an essay topic:*

The aftermath of 7/7 forces us to assess where we are. And here is where I think we are: we are sleepwalking our way to segregation. We are becoming strangers to each other, and we are leaving communities to be marooned outside the mainstream. (Trevor Phillips 22/9/05 Commission for Racial Equality – speech to Manchester Council for Community Relations)

Discuss.

Search for appropriate books, websites and journal articles using relevant keywords.

Chapter 8
Presentation

Possibly even before you start working as a qualified social worker you may be required to deliver a short presentation to senior managers as part of the interview process. PowerPoint can make this presentation look slick and professional, acting as an aide memoire to cover for your nerves. Social work is a varied career and does not just involve direct client contact or working within the statutory sector. You may be involved with community-based groups such as carers' groups who occasionally may require slightly more formal presentation of ideas. Similarly, you may be asked to give a presentation on an aspect of your service to interested stakeholders who may be responsible for allocating additional funds to keep your project afloat. With the intro- duction of the GSCC registration requirements to demonstrate ongoing professional development, social workers now have to undertake additional study which may well involve group presentations. A well-structured PowerPoint presentation combined with handouts is guaranteed to hold people's interest far better than a collection of scrappy notes that have the potential to get out of order, or worse still, lost. PowerPoint also has sophisticated editing abilities and therefore can be used to create cards, posters and flyers.

Getting started

There are a number of commercially available presentation packages that you may be familiar with already, such as Lotus Freelance Graphics or Corel Presentation 9. For the purposes of the ECDL you need to become competent in using Microsoft PowerPoint. This can be accessed via the icon shown in Figure 8.1.

Figure 8.1

You will then get directed to the 'Normal View' of PowerPoint which consists of the 'Outline View' area on the left-hand side of the screen, the 'Slide View' area in the main part of the screen, and the 'Notes View' at the bottom of the screen. See the example in Figure 8.2.

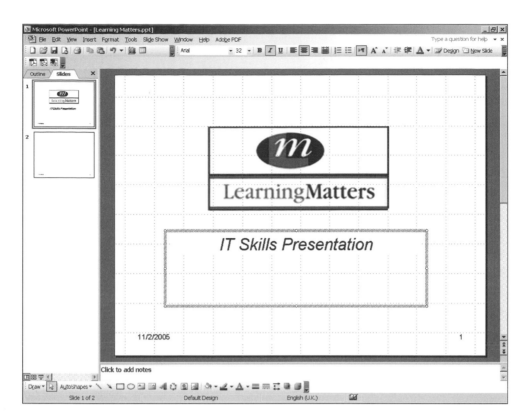

Figure 8.2

You will also see a pop-up menu which will invite you to select whether or not you wish to open an existing presentation, use the Autocontent Wizard to create a new presentation, use a 'Design template' or simply start a new blank presentation from scratch. Design templates are pre-saved templates that you can use to add interest and colour to your presentation rather than simply typing monochrome text onto slides.

As with other Microsoft software applications, many of the functions you will need to use to create a basic presentation can be accessed either via the pull-down menus at the top of the screen or by double-clicking on the short-cut icons in the toolbar. The 'File' menu has all of the usual options you would expect to find and if you access 'Print' from this menu you can choose to have either your slides printed, or handouts for your audience.

You can switch views by either clicking on the icons in the bottom left of your screen which represent the different views, or by selecting the 'View' pull-down menu. The 'Slide Sorter' is a useful tool to be able to use, especially when you are working on a presentation of more than five slides. It enables you to see all of the slides on one screen and alter their order, delete them, add additional slides, or simply hide selected slides when creating a slide presentation.

The 'Insert' menu allows you to add new slides as well as inserting pictures or graphics from other files. As with Excel, you can add a chart or table directly into your presentation without having to export it from another application. This can also be achieved by double-clicking on the chart or table icon on the toolbar. You can also add in slides from existing presentations to the one that you are working on.

Although all of the slides in a presentation have to be in the same landscape or portrait format, they can all have different layouts. The default layout is for a title at the top of the slide and then bullet points in the main body. However, if you click on the 'Format' pull-down menu you can choose to alter the layout of your slide from this default option. Other formats include completely blank slides, a title page, two columns of bullet points and combinations of charts, graphics and text.

You will notice that PowerPoint has a pull-down menu that you will not find in any of the other applications covered so far. This is the 'Slideshow' menu and this enables you to create stand-alone 'shows' of your slides with the presentation running automatically without an operator to prompt slide changes. This menu also allows you to insert 'transitional effects' such as text spiralling onto the screen to the sound of applause.

Presentations can be as simple or as complex as you like, but do remember that the presentation is ultimately being created for an audience other than yourself. Whilst you may like to show off all of the new skills that you have learned within PowerPoint, too many special effects may end up confusing the message that you are intending to convey to your audience.

Have a go now at Activities 8.1–8.8.

Activity 8.1	*Preparing a new presentation*

1. *Open up PowerPoint and start to create a new presentation.*
2. *Title your presentation 'Core Skills of Social Work' and with the subtitle 'Service Users' Expectations'.*
3. *Create six slides for the following key expectations (taken from TOPSS National Occupational Standards for Social worker 'Statement of Expectations':* **www.topssengland.net/files/cd/England/Expect.htm***):*
   - *Communication Skills and Information Sharing*
   - *Good Social Work Practice*
   - *Advocacy*
   - *Working with Other Professionals*
   - *Knowledge*
   - *Values.*
4. *Change the font so that each of the slides utilises a different one e.g. the title page is in Arial, slide 2 is Comic Sans MS, etc.*
5. *On each of the Expectations slides, insert a large WordArt number behind the text, e.g. the slide with 'Advocacy' on it will have the number 3 behind it, as in Figure 8.3.*

Figure 8.3

6. Go to the web address provided above and, using the information there, add additional slides after each of those already created. Title each additional slide with the Expectation and then include bullet points to provide the detail, e.g. for the slide titled 'Communication Skills and Information Sharing' you will need to add bullet points a–l. As this will make your slide look very crowded, you will need to add more than one additional slide for each Expectation.

7. Create a final slide with the website reference for TOPSS given above.

8. Save your presentation as 'Statement of Expectations' in your IT Skills folder.

9. Create a separate presentation of just the original seven slides by hiding the additional slides added in parts 6 and 7 of this activity. View this as a slideshow.

10. Create a printout of all of your slides.

Activity *8.2*   *Preparing a presentation using a design template*

1. Create a new PowerPoint presentation entitled 'Key Legislation for Social Workers' and use a design template such as 'Dad's Tie' or 'Cactus'. The range of templates on offer will vary depending on which version of Windows you are using.

2. Create a title slide with 'Key Legislation for Social Workers' as the main title and your name as the subtitle.

3. Create the four slides using the blank slide and title format. Title the slides:
    a. Children
    b. People with Learning Disabilities
    c. People with Mental Health Difficulties
    d. Older People.

3. Add bullet points of key pieces of legislation with regards to each group; e.g. for children you might include the Children Act 1989 and the Adoption and Children Act 2002.

4. Create a fifth slide with a title and table format. Title this slide 'Other Key Legislation'. Create a table with the following information in it:

Human Rights Act 1998	Allows individuals to pursue their human rights within UK courts
Freedom of Information Act 2000	Gives individuals the right to request information held by a public authority
Data Protection Act 1998	Requires LA to inform clients that informati,on is held electronically about them and gives clients the right to access this information
Care Standards Act 2000	Requires the registration of all social workers and provides for the protection of title 'social worker'

5. Now create one final slide entitled 'The importance of understanding legislation'. List at least four reasons with numbered bullet points.

6. Save the presentation in your IT Skills folder and create handouts for your audience.

Activity *8.3*   *Inserting other files into a presentation*

1. Create a new PowerPoint presentation entitled 'Carers: The Role of Social Work'. Use a different design template to the one used in the presentation in the previous activity.
2. Create six slides with the following headings:

   a. Definition of Carer

   b. Policy Guidance

   c. Key Legislation

   d. What Services can Social Services provide?

   e. Relevant Support Agencies – locally

   f. Relevant Support Agencies – nationally.

3. Go online and find the relevant information to add to each of the slides – if you are unsure where to look, visit **www.carersuk.org or http://www.carers.gov.uk/**
4. Save your presentation, print it out as either slides or handouts and close the file.
5. Open up your presentation on 'Key Legislation for Social Workers'. Insert the slide on legislation for Carers into this presentation after the slide on Older People. Make sure that the inserted slide now has the same formatting as the other slides in the presentation.
6. Save and print out handouts with six slides to a page.

Activity *8.4*   *Altering an existing presentation*

1. Open your PowerPoint File 'Key Legislation for Social Workers'.
2. Change the title page to 'Understanding the Law' and alter the sub-heading to 'PowerPoint Presentation'.
3. Delete 'Freedom of Information Act' from the fifth slide.
4. Delete the slide 'The Importance of Understanding Legislation'.
5. Add a final slide titled 'References' to provide a bibliography of books and other resources on social work law. Change the design template to a different one.
6. Save your amended PowerPoint presentation in your IT Skills folder and print out some handouts for your audience.

Activity *8.5*	*Printing handouts with notes*

1. *Utilising either your own PowerPoint presentation or the existing one referred to in the previous activity, add some explanatory notes to the bottom of each slide. This will act as an aide memoire if you have to deliver the presentation to an audience.*
2. *Add your own name and date as a footer for the handout view – make sure that these only appear on each page of the handout, not on each slide. Include the page number in the bottom right-hand corner of the handout.*
3. *Create and print handouts that include your notes at the bottom of the page.*

Example:

Slide 1

> # How is Social work different from the role of other Social Care and Health Professionals?

Get the group to break Into pairs to consider this. Allow about 10 minutes to allow a good discussion.
Issues that I want to raise include: differing value bases/training/length of education/value that society places on social workers/medical v social models of care/status.
Fariah Seppideh 1/6/05

Activity *8.6*	*Using special effects*

1. *Create a new presentation or open one of the existing PowerPoint files that you have already worked on.*
2. *You will now need to add some transitional effects to the presentation in order to make it more audience-friendly. Examples could include:*
   - *each new slide appearing letter by letter onto the screen;*
   - *each new slide arriving with the accompaniment of a sound clip such as a round of applause;*
   - *each new line of text on a slide appearing using a 'blinds' effect.*
4. *Save your presentation in your IT Skills folder.*

Activity 8.7   *Creating a slideshow*

1. Create a new presentation called 'My Placement' or 'My Workplace' using a design template.
2. If possible, include the logo or letterhead design of your placement provider or employer on the title page.
3. Create five slides on the following topics:
   - Client Group and Eligibility Criteria
   - Mission Statement
   - Work Undertaken – use two bullet-point columns for this
   - Team Members – use an organisational chart for this
   - Contact Details.
4. Add some transitional effects as well as timings to your presentation so that each slide automatically appears without requiring a mouse click.
5. Save your presentation as a stand-alone slideshow in your IT Skills folder.
6. E-mail your slideshow to a friend to watch. They should be able to watch the slideshow without opening up PowerPoint on their computer.

Activity 8.8   *Creating a greetings card using PowerPoint*

1. Create a new presentation and save it as 'Congratulations'.
2. Using the blank slide format in portrait view, type 'Congratulations on achieving your Degree!' in the top left-hand corner of the page (this will become the inside of the card when it is folded correctly in four).
3. Reformat the text to a user-friendly font and use a different colour if your printer will support this.
4. Rotate the text by 180° so that it is upside down. This will then appear the right way up when you fold the paper.
5. Now create a suitable front for your card using an image from ClipArt and a WordArt 'Congratulations'. This will need to be positioned in the bottom right-hand corner of the page.
6. On the reverse of your card (the bottom left-hand corner) type a small '© <<Your Name>> <<Date>>'. You can use the gridlines to assist with positioning this accurately.
7. Print out a copy of your card. See Figure 8.4 for an example of how it might look.

Figure 8.4

Chapter 9
Internet and e-mail

Introduction

Knowledge of e-mail systems and the Internet is an essential skill for any individual in the 21st century, let alone a social worker. A considerable proportion of communication between the social worker, management team and other professionals will come via the e-mail system and therefore it is vital to be conversant with basic functions. These include regularly emptying your Inbox so that your system does not get clogged and slow down to a grinding halt.

Service users are well aware of the potential of the Internet and there is no longer any excuse for social workers to be ill-informed about obscure medical conditions or the latest benefits rates. As the well-known saying goes, knowledge is power, and this applies to service users as well. The Internet contains a wealth of information and makes it comparatively easy for individuals to keep abreast of the latest research into treatment, therapies and adaptations. Service users can equip themselves with far more information than was previously possible before going to see their GP or consultant and therefore gain a better understanding of potential options available to them.

However, a cautionary note needs to be sounded. Anyone can host a web page and sometimes material contained on them can be very damaging, especially for vulnerable individuals. For example, there are numerous websites about suicide and self-harm. The majority offer support and advice on how to overcome suicidal feelings. However, a number offer ideas on how to successfully commit suicide. Just because information is posted on the Internet, it does not mean to say that it is true. Therefore, it is vital that social workers are able to carefully evaluate the reliability and authenticity of information gathered from the Web in order to ensure that it is accurate. Bear in mind the following points when evaluating material:

- Who hosts the website? Is it a recognised organisation such as Help the Aged, Department of Health, or Office for National Statistics?
- Who sponsors the website? For example, if you are trying to get accurate information on smoking-related diseases, a website sponsored by a tobacco company may not provide you with unbiased research.
- When was the web page last updated? Just because you are accessing the information in 2006 does not mean to say that the material is up to date.
- If it is an article, has it been peer-reviewed or published elsewhere in hard copy? Is it evidence-based?
- Is the material relevant to the UK context?

The Internet Social Worker (Activity 9.5) is an invaluable tool for social workers and will assist you further in evaluating material that you find on the web.

The Internet is also frequently the breeding ground for many viruses and therefore it is important to be aware of the security implications of attaching and sending information to colleagues and others via e-mail. At worst, a virus can render your computer unusable, which could be a very costly mistake if it is your own personal computer at home. If you are ever unsure about an e-mail, do not reply to it or open the attachments. If the sender is genuine, they will probably follow it up with another e-mail or a telephone call to ask for a response.

Getting started

The ECDL requires you to have knowledge of Internet Explorer which can be accessed via the icon shown in Figure 9.1.

Figure 9.1

Double-clicking on this icon will connect you to the Internet if you are not already connected. Once connected you will be automatically directed to your Internet 'home page', which could be MSN Search, your university or work's website or a website of your choice (you can choose what to have as your home page via the Control Panel). Irrespective of the web page filling the main part of your screen, you will see the toolbar illustrated in Figure 9.2.

Figure 9.2

This toolbar will help you to navigate your way around the Internet. The arrow icons will allow you to go back and forwards through web pages rather like you would flick through the pages of a book. The house icon will return you automatically to your 'home page', whilst the magnifying glass 'Search' icon will allow you to search the Internet for a specific topic or website using MSN Search. If you already know the address of the website that you wish to visit, then you can type it directly into the 'Address Bar' and click on the 'Go' icon. Website addresses generally have at least three components separated by full-stops, e.g.

www.	yahoo.	com

This is known as its URL (universal resource locator) and you will frequently see web addresses with easily recognisable extensions, e.g. **www.dh.gov.uk** is the URL for the Department of Health in the UK.

If you don't know the web address of the site that you are looking for, or wish to carry out a general search for information on a specific topic, then you would use a 'search engine'. This is basically a program that is able to search the World Wide Web for information that matches your search criteria. Popular UK search engines include Google (**www.google.co.uk**), Altavista (**www.altavista.co.uk**) and Lycos (**www.lycos.co.uk**).

For websites that you visit frequently there is the option of adding them to your 'Favorites'. This means that with one click you can go directly to the website, without having to either remember the address or go via the lengthy route of locating it using a search engine. Within Internet Explorer, you will see the pull-down menu option 'Favorites' with a 'Star' icon next to it. If you click on this you will see a list of all of the favourites that the computer has already compiled for you. To add your own websites, click on 'Add' and you can simply type in the web address, click on 'OK' and then it will be added to your list of favourites. This is also sometimes known as 'bookmarking' your websites.

There are many web-based e-mail services available free on the Internet, such as Hotmail or Yahoo!Mail, and you may also be familiar with a web-based mail tool at university. However, the ECDL also requires you to be competent in using the e-mail software package Microsoft Outlook. Once you are connected to the Internet, you can access Outlook via the icon shown in Figure 9.3.

Figure 9.3

You will then be directed to the main Outlook screen, which basically consists of a toolbar at the top, a shortcut bar on the left, and, provided that you are in the 'Inbox' view, your incoming e-mails in the main pane, as in Figure 9.4.

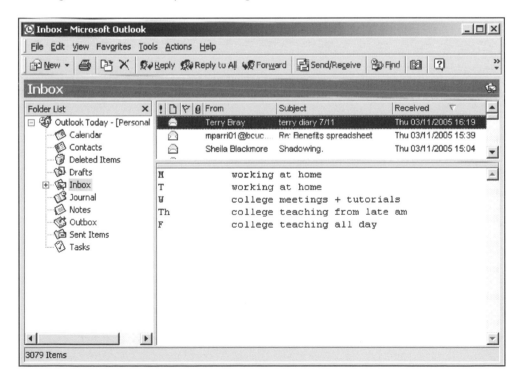

Figure 9.4

You can move between views by clicking on the options on the left-hand side of the screen, but mainly you will be working from the Inbox.

In order to send an e-mail, click on 'New' on the toolbar. A blank e-mail form will then appear for you to work from. You will need to know the e-mail address of the person you wish to communicate with and e-mail addresses are easily distinguishable from Internet web page addresses as they contain the symbol @. Type in the name of the recipient into the 'To' box and if you wish to send the e-mail to more than one person, you need to separate out each address using a semi-colon, e.g.

tonyblair@no10.gov.uk; gordonbrown@no11.gov.uk

Remember to include a 'Subject', as some mail servers reject e-mails as 'Spam' (unwanted and unsolicited junk e-mail) and therefore your intended recipient may not get to see your e-mail.

If you want to send a copy of a Word document or any other electronic file, you can do this by 'attaching' it to your e-mail. To do this, you need to click on 'Insert' from the pull-down menu and then click on 'Insert File'. A pop-up menu will then appear asking you where the file is stored. You can browse your computer drives in order to find the file and then click on 'Attach'. The pop-up menu will then close and you will return to your draft e-mail. You should see a little icon appear with the file name next to it indicating that the file has been successfully attached. To send the e-mail, click on 'Send'.

In order to read e-mails that have been sent to you, simply click on the relevant e-mail. It doesn't matter if you click on the e-mail's subject or author, both will allow you to view the message. If you wish to reply to the e-mail, then click on 'Reply' from the toolbar at the top of the screen. This will automatically generate the recipient's e-mail address in a new message form, and it will often include the original e-mail in your reply. You may also wish to forward on an e-mail to a third party. To do this, simply open up the e-mail and then click on 'Forward'. You will then be required to enter the new recipient's e-mail address. Remember though that just because you find an email interesting, relevant or amusing, your intended recipient may not!

You are now ready to complete the final activities in this book.

Activity **9.1**	*Filling in an online form*

1. *Log on to the Community Care Magazine website:*
   www.communitycare.co.uk.
2. *Click on 'Subscribe' and fill in the online form to apply to subscribe free to the magazine.*
   (This weekly magazine for social workers is essential reading and will be invaluable for your studies.)

Activity 9.2 — Using a search engine

1. Log on to the Internet and start using the search engine Google.
2. Search the Net to find a chart depicting the finger-spelling alphabet for deaf people. Copy the chart into a Word document and save in your ECDL folder, indicating the web reference as your source.
3. Now see if you can find the British Sign Language (BSL) signs for 'homework' and 'school'. You should be able to locate a video clip for this.
4. Now search the Net for British Sign Language courses delivered at Level 1 in your local area.
5. Print the results of all your searches.

Activity 9.3 — Sending an e-mail with an attachment

1. Open up your e-mail program and create a new message to send to a close friend or family member.
2. Attach a high-priority flag to your message.
3. Type in the following message, including all spelling mistakes:

> Dear <<Your friend's name>>
>
> As you know I am tring to improve my computr skills and practising by using a Learning Matters workbook. One of the excercises involves snending an e-mail to a friend – hence my e-mail to you! I have to send an atachment and have therefore sent you a Word document. Could you e-mail me back to confirm that you have received the document and been able to open it ok?
>
> Thanks!
>
> << Your name>>

4. Now carry out a spell check on your e-mail before attaching a recent Word document that you are happy to share with your friend.
5. Send the e-mail and await the reply, which you can then print out to include in your portfolio.

Activity 9.4 — Inserting a hyperlink

1. Log on to the Internet and start using the search engine Google.
2. Search the Net for an unusual website that you think might be of interest to a friend – it really can be anything (although clearly nothing that will land either you or your friend on the wrong side of the Criminal Justice system!)
3. E-mail the web address as a hyperlink to your friend and ask them to confirm that they were able to access the site via your e-mail.
4. Print out a copy of your e-mail conversation.

Activity 9.5	Using the Internet

1. Log on to the website **www.vts.rdn.ac.uk/tutorial/social-worker**.

2. *Work your way through the site (see Figure 9.5) and make sure that you familiarise yourself with the jargon and concepts discussed. The websites that it will signpost you to will be invaluable for your assignments over the course of your social work education.*

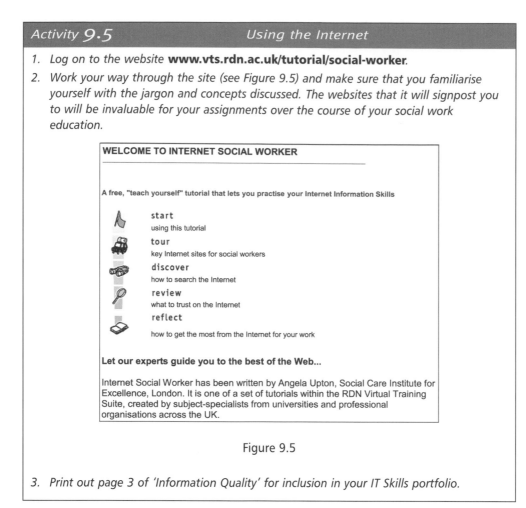

Figure 9.5

3. *Print out page 3 of 'Information Quality' for inclusion in your IT Skills portfolio.*

Activity 9.6	Contributing to an online discussion

1. *Log on to* **www.socialwork-students.com/index.php** *and access one of the forums that are currently live (see Figure 9.6). If this is your first time of visiting the site, you will need to register (which is free).*

2. *Bookmark this site, i.e. add it to your 'Favorites'.*

3. *Select a relevant forum topic that is of interest to you and then add a comment yourself. Try to make sure that it is adding something to the discussion or you will end up alienating yourself from the rest of the discussion board and social work student community!*

4. *Print a copy of your contribution to the discussion board. This should preferably contain a reply from one of your peers.*

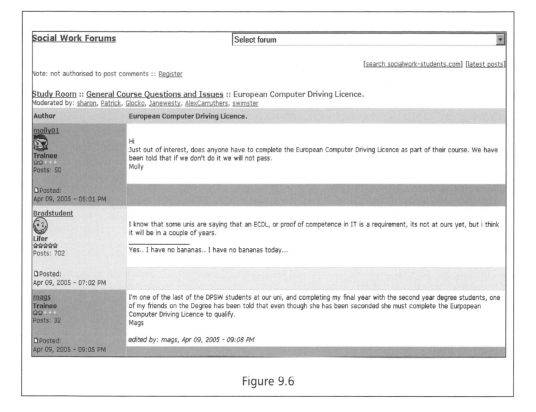

Figure 9.6

Activity 9.7 — Downloading media clips

1. Go to **www.imagesofdisability.gov.uk/broadcast.asp**. You will need to do this exercise on a machine that has the capacity to support the playing of media clips and will need either *Windows Media Player*, *RealPlayer* or *QuickTime* installed (the latter two programs are available free of charge and can be downloaded from the above site).

2. Watch the video clip of the interview with the man who reveals a history of depression. What prejudiced actions or remarks does the interviewer make?

3. Now watch the video clip of 'Committee'. What is the slogan of this clip?

4. If you have time, watch the remaining video clips in the series. Save one of the clips as a Movie Clip in your IT Skills folder.

Activity 9.8   *Saving and forwarding web-based information*

1. *Log on to the website* Research Mindedness in Social Work and Social Care
   www.resmind.swap.ac.uk/content/02_what_is/what_is_01_01.htm

2. *Complete the online self-assessment form (Figure 9.7) to find out how research-minded you are. Take note of the results.*

Assessment questions	Not at all	Partly	Very well
I understand the importance and relevance of research to social work practice	○	○	◉
I understand the broad principles involved in research	○	◉	○
I understand the ethical issues involved in research	○	◉	○
I know how to access, understand and summarise research studies	○	◉	○
I know how to make use of anti-oppressive perspectives in evaluating research and practice	○	○	◉
I know how to identify research which is relevant to practice in which I am involved	◉	○	○
I know how to relate research to practice issues and demonstrate how relevant research informs practice	◉	○	○

 Completed   Questions not answered will be treated as 'Not at all'.   Reset

Figure 9.7

3. *E-mail the completed table (not the following results page) to your dissertation supervisor or tutor if you have one. Save your completed form in your IT Skills folder as well.*

4. *Now work your way through the web pages which will provide you with a wealth of information and advice on how to search for up-to-date research on the Web. This will not only assist you with your dissertation, but also all your other written assignments.*

Concluding remarks

You have now reached the end of the activities in the book. Congratulations if you have managed to complete all of them successfully! You should now have an impressive portfolio of IT skills to show either to future or current employers, or simply to boost your own confidence in your ability to use computers. By working through the activities you should now feel confident to tackle most Microsoft applications, and, as with social work itself, the skills that you have learned are transferable. Therefore, you should now feel comfortable with navigating your way around most menu-based software applications and hopefully feel less daunted by new database systems and technology when introduced into the workplace.

In addition to learning practically about how to use a personal computer, this book has also encouraged you to think about the ethical implications of IT in social care. Social workers are required to continually reflect on their practice which involves an increasing reliance on modern technology and ever diminishing amount of time being spent on face-to-face contact with service users. Whilst it is clearly important to feel competent and relaxed about using a computer, competence should not come at the expense of considering the potential impact of using a computer to record sensitive information.

As illustrated in the introduction, IT skills are becoming a familiar request in job specifications for social workers and updating these skills can no longer be something that can be put on the back-burner. The General Social Care Council requires computer literacy as a prerequisite for gaining a degree in professional social work. However, IT does not stand still and software applications are continually being upgraded and adapted to have even more functions. Therefore, working on your IT skills is an essential part of continuous professional development after you qualify. As a condition of continuing registration with the General Social Care Council, you need to demonstrate over a three year period at least ninety hours (15 days) of study related to professional development. The guidelines as to what constitutes appropriate study are left deliberately open to encompass a wide range of activities that will benefit your current employment, your career progression and form part of your wider professional development (GSCC: 2006). Therefore, if you are contemplating applying for a managerial position that requires you to manage budgets as part of your everyday work, you could reasonably include a course of advanced training on Microsoft Excel as part of your study time.

Learning to use a computer is rather like learning to drive. By completing the activities, you will now have achieved a basic level of competence across a wide range of IT applications. However, in order to become truly competent, you now need to practice more, and explore the full potential of the software packages. The activities were designed to introduce you to the key tools of each Microsoft software application, but there are many more tools contained within the packages for you to discover. By using this book, you will be familiar with the Help functions, tool bars and pull-down menus of each application. Be curious; ask colleagues, IT support staff, family and friends about how they use the computer. Often you can learn quick time-saving short-cuts from other people through a brief demonstration if you are prepared to invest a bit of time in enhancing your IT skills. The challenge for you now is to build upon what you already know and utilise the full potential of the computer to help you in both your professional and personal life.

Happy computing!

IT courses

If you do not feel confident teaching yourself the required skills to complete all of the activities within this portfolio, many local colleges offer low-cost computing courses. Many of the courses are available as evening classes. You can also sign up to LearnDirect: **http://catalogue.learndirect.co.uk/browse/usingit/**. Alternatively, if you think that you might learn best through the use of an interactive CD-ROM, you can purchase one through AdvanceLearning: **www.advancelearning.com/uk/orderCdOnline.php**.

Recommended coursebooks

If you feel that you learn best through working on your own using a book for guidance, you may find the following texts helpful:

- Bessant, A (2004a) *Learning to Pass ECDL Syllabus 4.0 for Office 2000*. Oxford: Heinemann

- Bessant, A (2004b) *Learning to Pass ECDL Syllabus 4.0 for Office XP*. Oxford: Heinemann

- The British Computer Society (2004) *ECDL/ICDL 4.0 Study Guide*. San Francisco: Sybex

- Holden, P and Munnelly, B (2003a) *How to Pass ECDL 4: Office 2000*. Harlow: Prentice Hall

- Holden, P and Munnelly, B (2003b) *ECDL4: The Complete Coursebook for Office XP*. Harlow: Prentice Hall

- Holden P and Munnelly, B (2003) *ECDL4: The Complete Coursebook for Microsoft Office 2000.* Harlow: Prentice Hall

- Moran, J, Hull, V and Wheeler, D (2003) *The Complete Idiot's Guide to ECDL.* London: Prentice Hall

Web-based social work resources

In addition to the exercises within this pack, you may like to further increase your confidence and computer literacy skills by exploring some of the following sites on the web.

1. **www.socialwork-students.com/index.php**
   This is a website run and maintained by a social work student at de Montfort University. You need to 'join' (free) and then are able to access a wealth of online articles and materials recommended by fellow students. There are also numerous discussion boards going, offering advice about a wide variety of social work student-related issues. It is approved by The British Association of Social Workers.

2. **www.socialwork.ed.ac.uk/Teaching/InteractivEAL/index.htm**
   This is a self-directed Enquiry and Action Learning set devised by the University of Edinburgh. It involves the use of two case studies – one criminal justice and one children and families. You work through the cases and have the opportunity to view media clips of other students' thoughts on possible interventions and theories for understanding the cases.
   Be aware that the law and some policies referred to relate to Scotland only and are not applicable in England.

3. **www.external.swap.ac.uk/socialworklaw/index.htm**
   This is a set of four interactive law tutorials devised by de Montfort University. The tutorials cover the following areas:

   - basic principles of law and practice with special reference to the law regarding discrimination and rights of redress;

   - law and practice as they relate to people needing community care services;

   - law and practice as they relate to people needing protection from abuse by others;

   - law and practice as they relate to people needing protection from themselves.

4. **www.sws.soton.ac.uk/cwab/index.htm**
   This is another interactive course whose intention is to promote the need for child welfare practitioners to act more effectively locally by thinking globally. It hasn't been updated since 2003 so some of the links may not work any more.

5. **www.hcc.uce.ac.uk/virtualplacement/About.htm**
   This is an interactive software package that is available as a free download. It is designed by Mark Doel and Tarsem Singh Cooner in order to prepare students and practice teachers for practice learning within a virtual environment, in this case, a wood.

6. **www2.rgu.ac.uk/publicpolicy/socialpolicy.htm**
   This is more of an informative website from Robert Gordon University that provides an accessible introduction to social policy, including content on social security, welfare and values.

7. **www.swap.ac.uk/shared/cardgame/card_game5.html**
   Another interactive website that allows you to play a version of the card game 'Patience' in order to consider key roles and learning opportunities prior to going out on placement. As there are no instructions on the link above, you will need to visit the following link for assistance:
   www.swap.ac.uk/elearning/webpool7.asp

8. **www.swap.ac.uk/Links/links.asp?sid=_Jacsa3**
   This is the Social Policy and Social Work (SWAP) website that has links to peer-reviewed websites relating to social work and social policy. It is invaluable to visit when seeking information and authoritative data to back up assignments.

9. **www.sosig.ac.uk/social_welfare/**
   Similar to the SWAP pages, the Social Sciences Information Gateway aims to provide a trusted source of selected, high-quality Internet information for researchers and practitioners in social work.

10. **www.resmind.swap.ac.uk/content/02_what_is/what_is_01_01.htm**
    Research mindedness in social work and social care is a website funded by the Social Care Institute for Excellence (SCIE), to help students and practitioners of social care and social work make greater and more effective use of research in their studies and in practice. N.B: it ceased to be updated in September 2005.

11. **www.vts.rdn.ac.uk/tutorial/social-worker**
    The Internet Social Worker tutorial is an interactive website designed to help people new to the internet make the most of the potential it offers.

12. **www.scie-socialcareonline.org.uk/**
    A free and easy to use web-based research database added to on a daily basis by researchers at SCIE.

13. **www.rip.org.uk/**
    This website promotes evidence-based practice in working with children and families. It is run by the Dartington Hall Trust in association with the Association of Directors of Social Services.

14. **www.jrf.org.uk/**
    This is the website of the Joseph Rowntree Foundation which seeks to undertake research into the causes of social problems. The research findings are invaluable for supporting evidence-based practice and inclusion in assignments.

Bibliography

Brammer, A (2003) *Social work law*. London: Macmillan

Computer Ethics Institute (1992) *Ten commandments of computer ethics.*
www.cpsr.org/issues/ethics/cei [accessed 27/7/05]

Glastonbury, B (1985) *Computers in social work*. Basingstoke: Macmillan

Glastonbury, B (1995) Risk, information technology and social care, *New Technology in the Human Services*, 8 (3), 2–10

GSCC (2002) *Accreditation of universities to grant degrees in social work.*
www.gscc.org.uk [accessed 12/4/04]

GSCC (2006) *Post-registration Training* **www.gscc.org.uk/Training+and+learning/ Continuing+your+training/Post-registration+training/**

Hampshire County Council (2005) *Senior practitioner job description.*
www3.hants.gov.uk/profile.htm?profile=50009780 [accessed 27/7/05]

Holt, J and Rafferty, J (2005) *Building skills into the curriculum: a guide to meeting the requirement for social work degree students to achieve information and communication technology skills*. SWAP **www.swap.ac.uk** [accessed 7/6/05]

Information Commissioner's Office (2005) *Data protection myths and realities.*
www.ico.gov.uk/cms/DocumentUploads/Data_Protection_Myths_and_ Realities_16_1_06_2.pdf

Lewis J and Glennerster, H (1996) *Implementing the new community care*. Milton Keynes: Open University Press

Postle, K (2002) *Working between the idea and the reality: ambiguities and tensions in care managers' work*, British Journal of Social Work, 32, 335–51

Sapey, B (1997) *Social work tomorrow: towards a critical understanding of computers in social work*, British Journal of Social Work, 27 (6), 803–814

SCIE (2003) Creating an e-learning strategy for social care in England.
www.scie.org.uk/publications/elearning.asp

TOPSS England (2002) National occupational standards for social workers
www.topssengland.net/view.asp?id=140 [accessed 20/7/05]

Model answers

These are based on Windows XP and OfficeXP. However, if you have an older version of either Windows or Office, you should still be able to work through these step-by-step guides. There may just be some slight differences in the display on the screen, or the options on offer at any given point. Older versions of Office do not have as many Wizards on offer.

Activity 3.1 Computer quiz

1. a. If a social worker is based at more than one office, they can still access their own files such as letters and reports and work on them.
    b. If there is an emergency/crisis and the allocated social worker is not available, some files/information can be shared across the network; e.g. if a report has been saved in a shared drive, workers other than the author can access it.
    c. Case notes can be shared on a common database used by social services or other agencies. These can be accessed by workers in different locations and means that information can be stored in just one 'virtual' place rather than in a series of paper files.
    d. Service users do not need to repeat key information to multiple members of staff as it can be readily accessed by the person accessing the computer database.

2. This promotes computer security so that sensitive information is protected and accessed only by those who have permission. The ***** prevents anyone standing close being able to see the password as it is being entered although, of course, they could still look at your fingers typing it in!

3. Microsoft Office Publisher can be used to produce newsletters and other material that utilises a mix of media such as photos/graphics/text. It allows the user to manipulate images and text to produce a professional-looking document. In a social work setting you could use it to create a promotional flyer for a group or for a team newsletter.

4. As computers are not infallible, it is essential to keep backup copies of important pieces of work/files. Backup copies are copies of files and these can be kept in a separate folder to the original (in order to prevent accidental editing or deletion of the original) or on a USB pen drive/CD-ROM. Social services generally create backups every evening of their database in order to mitigate against virus infiltration or accidental destruction of vital work.

5. a. You could 'contract' a computer virus by using an infected floppy disk or trying to open a file on your USB pen drive that has already been corrupted on another computer.
    b. Another way that you could contract a virus is by opening an infected e-mail. Often viruses are detected by sophisticated anti-virus software and will be deleted before they even enter your in-box. To reduce the risk of catching a virus this way, see if you recognise the sender of the e-mail first. If there is an attachment that you are unsure about, don't open it as this could result in your computer becoming infected.

    c. You could also contract a virus by downloading material from non-secure sites. This is a problem particularly associated with illegal downloads of music files.

6. *This is an Act that protects people against companies or other individuals misusing their personal information that is stored on a computer. This means that all companies holding personal information must be registered and must notify individuals that they will be storing information electronically. The implications for social care are that all agencies should make service users aware at the point of first contact that their details are stored on a computer system.*

7. *System software helps to run your computer. An example of this would be the operating system or the printer applications. Application software helps you to undertake specific activities such as spreadsheets, databases and word processors.*

8. *a. E-mail*
   b. Home shopping via the Internet
   c. Internet banking
   d. Programming video/DVD to record a programme
   e. Correspondence
   f. Filing tax return
   g. Downloading music

9. *GUI stands for Graphical User Interface. This represents files, programs and functions as pictures on the screen. These are the icons, windows and images that most modern users have grown up with. Previously you would have had to either enter in code, or use the function keys at the top of the keyboard.*
   a. It is more user-friendly in that you can have a pull-down menu that clearly tells the user how to select various options.
   b. You do not have to remember what the various function buttons (F1–12) at the top of the keyboard mean.
   c. You can have several applications open in different windows running at the same time.

10. *a. E-mail – requires a computer*
    b. Fax
    c. Telephone/minicom

11. *Disk drives you may come across are the hard disk, the network drive, floppy disk, CD-ROM and pen drive.*

12. *USB pen drives have the advantage that they are i) cheap, ii) portable, iii) can be used as backup copies.*

13. *a. Taking regular breaks to reduce eye strain and back problems*
    b. Using a wrist rest
    c. Positioning the screen to avoid glare from a window or other light source
    d. Having a comfortable and supportive chair
    e. Using a document holder.

14. *a. Networked system across the authority to ensure that a social worker can access relevant data in whichever office they are working*
    b. Client database to share key information about clients such as basic details (name, address, etc.) as well as case recording (details of visits, risks, etc.)
    c. Spreadsheets to help with budget management.

15. The central processing unit runs everything within your computer, as the name suggests. Its speed is measured in megahertz – MHz or in gigahertz – GHz.

16. If left near a magnetic field, the data will be erased. Similarly, if liquid is spilled on them, or if they are left in a damp or hot environment, the data could become corrupted.

17. a. It is cheaper
    b. It is a more efficient use of workers' time as e-mails can be sent at any time and be responded to virtually immediately if necessary
    c. Greater numbers of people can be reached, e.g. one e-mail could reach the entire organisation
    d. It saves paper.

18. A 'dumb' terminal would be something like the computers that you use in a library that only allow you to access the book catalogue, or an IT tourist information point in a town centre. You can extract information from them, but you cannot add new information and they will have limited application. An 'intelligent' terminal is a computer that is able to interact more, e.g. you can input information, it will be processed, saved, reformatted etc. Intelligent terminals can be used for a wide range of applications and can communicate with other terminals on the network, or utilise the World Wide Web.

19. A laptop or notepad.

    a. It is easily portable and therefore generally speaking lighter than a regular PC
    b. It incorporates an integral mouse
    c. It is not networked
    d. It can run off a battery and does not need to be connected to the mains.

20. Input devices include keyboard, scanner, mouse, Webcam, microphone. Output devices include printer, speakers, monitor. The printer works by receiving data from the computer and turning it into a 'hard' copy. The screen displays data that has already been converted from binary code into characters that are readily recognisable by the operator. The speakers similarly project audio data that has been converted from binary code.

Activity 4.1   Using the Control Panel

1. From the desktop, click on 'Start' in the bottom left-hand side of the screen. Select 'Settings' and then 'Control Panel'. Select 'Accessibility Options' by double-clicking on it.

2. A pop-up box will appear. Click on the 'Sound' tab and then click in the box 'Use SoundSentry'. Choose a visual warning 'Flash Action Caption Bar'. Click on 'Apply'. Re-select 'Accessibility Options'.

3. Click on the 'Display' tab. Then in 'Cursor Options' click and drag the arrow along the 'Blink Rate' scale towards 'None'. Repeat on the 'Width' scale in order to make the Cursor wider. Click on 'Apply'.

4. You should now be back in the main Control Panel menu. Click on the 'Display' option. A pop-up box will appear. Click on the 'Appearance' tab and then in the 'Color Scheme' box click on the pull-down menu arrow. Select 'High Contrast #1'. Click on 'Apply' and then 'OK'.

5. Close the Control Panel by going to the 'File' pull-down menu and clicking on 'Close'.

If you want to undo all of the above alterations (after you have checked to see how they work), repeat the above steps, uncheck the SoundSentry box, re-position the cursor arrows and select 'Windows Standard' or 'Windows XP' for the display screen colour scheme.

Activity 4.2   Using the Task Manager

1. Once you have opened up all of your files and have them displayed on the task bar at the bottom of the screen, hold down the 'Ctrl', 'Alt' and 'Delete' keys at the same time. This will pop-up the Task Manager menu.

2. The following box should appear (Figure A.1) showing you which applications are currently running on your computer. If one of your programs has frozen, it will tell you here that the program is 'not responding'. If this is the case, you can highlight that particular program by moving your cursor to it and highlighting it and then clicking on the 'End Task' button.

Figure A.1

3. Highlight each program opened individually and click on 'End Task'. You can also shut down your computer completely from the Task Manager by clicking on the 'Shutdown' tab.

Activity 4.3   File management

1. Open Word.
2. Go to 'File' (or the 'Open' tool button) and open any of your .doc files.
3. Once the file is open, click on 'Save as' A pop-up box will appear. Create a new folder by clicking on the 'Create New Folder' icon in the top right corner of the box.
4. Type in a name for your new folder, e.g. IT Skills. Click on 'OK'. The folder will now appear with no files saved in it. Type in the name of your document into the 'File' box. Click on 'Save'.

5. *In order to create a header/footer with the file directory showing, go to the toolbar and select 'View'.*

6. *Select 'Header/Footer'. The cursor will then flash in the dashed line box at the top of the screen. If you would rather insert a footer, move the cursor to the box at the bottom of the screen.*

7. *Select 'Insert Autotext' and 'Filename and Path' (Figure A.2).*

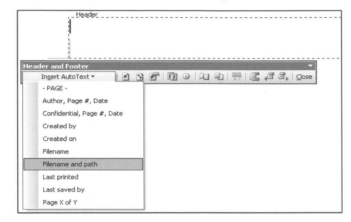

Figure A.2

8. *Close the toolbar and you should now be able to see a Header/Footer with a file directory showing, e.g.:*

   E:\My Documents\Personal Development\IT Skills\File Management.doc

   This indicates that the file is saved on the E drive (in this case, my USB pen drive), in the main folder 'Personal Development', sub-folder 'IT Skills', and is called 'File Management.doc'.

Activity *4.4*   Navigating your computer

1. *Exit and close down all applications that you have been working on and ensure that all of your data has been saved. Go to the 'Start' menu and click to 'Shut Down' your computer. You should not simply reach for the 'Off' button as this could lose your computer's settings as well as some of your unsaved data.*

2. *If you have one window taking up the full space of your screen, then you click in the top right-hand corner on the middle button, which will then resize your screen and make it smaller. If you then want to make the screen bigger (but not full size) you move your cursor to the bottom right-hand corner where there are three diagonal lines and drag the screen to the size you require. If you wish to reposition the screen, click and drag on the top blue bar.*

3. *Task Manager. Press the 'Ctrl', 'Alt' and 'Delete' keys at the same time in order to bring up the task menu. From here you can check to see which of your programmes has frozen. If one of your applications is 'Not responding' then you can simply close that one down rather than being forced to switch off the entire computer.*

4. *Double-click on 'My Computer' on the Desktop, then click on 'View System Information'. Alternatively go into 'Settings' via the 'Start' menu and select the 'Control*

Panel'. You can then click on the 'System'. A typical specification for a PC could be: Intel (R) Pentium (R)4 CPU 2.80 GHz, 512 MB of RAM.

5. You can either go to the 'Start' menu and click on 'Settings', then 'Control Panel' and then 'Display', or you can right-click on the Desktop and select 'Active Desktop', 'Customise My Desktop' and then when the Desktop pop-up menu appears click on the 'Screen Saver' button.

6. .doc needs Word, .jpg needs a photo-editing package such as Adobe Photoshop or Microsoft Photo editor, .xls requires Excel and .pdf requires Adobe Acrobat Reader.

7. You may have a HP/Canon/Lexmark printer showing when you go into 'Printer settings' via the 'Start' menu. In order to add an additional printer, you need to click on 'Add a Printer' and follow the instructions. In order to set a printer as your default printer you need to highlight which printer you wish to use. Then click on 'File' and select 'Set as Default Printer'.

8. Go into the 'Control Panel' via the 'Start' menu and select the 'Keyboard'. You will then see a sliding bar which you can adjust to alter the speed of the blink rate of the cursor.

9. Generally speaking you will have the Calculator, Wordpad, Paint and Address book.

10. When you choose to save your document, select the 'Save As' option from the 'File' menu. At the top of the box that pops up, you will see the task bar says 'Save in' and then it has a pull-down menu for you to select where you wish to save the document. Select the Desktop and then save. You will be able to check that it has been saved on the Desktop as it will appear on the Desktop as an icon.

Activity 4.5 — *Creating sub-folders*

1. Open Windows Explorer – this may be a separate icon on your desktop represented by a picture of a magnifying glass and a folder, or you may need to access it via the 'Start menu'.

2. You will see a pane on the left-hand side of the screen titled 'Folders'. If you click on 'My Computer' you will see all of the drives your computer has. Click on the relevant drive, e.g. System (C:) if you saved your IT Skills folder on the hard drive. You will then get a further layer of options. Keep selecting the relevant one, e.g. Documents and Settings, until you locate your folder.

3. If you do not know where you have saved it, click on the 'Search' icon on your tool bar. This will then ask you to identify that it is a 'File/Folder' that you are searching for and then requires you to enter the name of the folder. Click on 'Search'.

4. You should now see your IT Skills folder identified in the main pane of the screen and it should have the file directory in the address bar, e.g.

    c:\My Documents\IT Skills Folder

5. Double-click anywhere on the IT Skills folder in order to open it. It may be empty if you have not saved any activities into it yet.

6. To create new sub-folders, click on 'File' from the pull-down menus, then 'New' and then 'Folder'.

7. You will see [New Folder] appear in the main pane with a flashing cursor. Delete the words 'New Folder' and replace with 'Basic Concepts'. Then click on 'Enter'. You have now created a sub-folder.

8. *Repeat for the other headings.*

9. *Create a screen dump by holding down 'Ctrl' and 'Print Screen' at the same time. Open up a blank Word document and 'paste' the screen dump in by either clicking on the 'Paste' icon or holding down 'Ctrl' + 'V'.*

10. *Print by clicking on the 'Print' icon.*

Activity *4.6*   *File management using Windows Explorer*

1. *Open Word by double-clicking on the icon. Go to 'File' and click on 'Save As..' Type in 'File Management' into the 'Filename' bar. Click on 'Save'. Close Word by clicking on the X in the top right-hand corner of the screen.*

2. *Open Windows Explorer as described above.*

3. *On the left side of the screen you should see 'My Computer' listed. Click on this to reveal all of your drives. If you are not sure in which drive you have saved your document, follow step 2 in the above activity.*

4. *Once you have located 'File Management' hold down 'Ctrl' and 'Print Screen' to create a screen dump (as in step 9 above).*

5. *Highlight the document 'File Management' by clicking with either the left or right button, but keep your finger on the button. This will enable you to 'drag' the file to its new location.*

6. *Keeping your file highlighted as above, drag the file to one of the other folders in the left side of the screen. When you have identified the correct folder, release your mouse finger. This will 'drop' the file in the new folder.*

7. *To check that it has been located in the new folder, double-click on it and you should be able to see the file there. To rename the document, right-click on the name to highlight it and reveal the pop-up menu. Select 'Rename'. Then overtype 'File Management' with 'Activity 4.6' and press Return. Your document has now been renamed.*

Activity *4.7*   *Creating shortcuts on the Desktop*

1. *Insert a CD into the CD drive.*

2. *Click on the 'Start' menu and select 'Settings', then 'Taskbar and Start Menu'.*

3. *Click on the 'Start Menu' tab then select 'Customise'. Click on the 'Add' button. A shortcut Wizard will then start.*

4. *Click on 'Browse' in order to locate your CD. You may need to click on 'My Computer' in order to reveal all of the drives. Highlight your CD drive and click.*

5. *Then click on 'Next'. Select the Start menu folder to place your shortcut in and then click on 'Next' again. You will then be invited to type in a name for your shortcut.*

6. *Click on 'Finish' to exit the Wizard and then click on 'OK'. Close all of the menu boxes by clicking on the X.*

7. *If you click on 'Start' now, you should see your CD as a shortcut and if you click on it, your CD will start to run (or if it is a music CD it will start to play using Windows Media).*

8. *To copy it to the Desktop, close down any other programs running. Click on 'Start' to reveal your newly created shortcut. Move your cursor over the CD shortcut and depress the left mouse button. Continue holding it down and then drag the icon to any position on the Desktop.*

9. *Release the mouse button. You have now created a shortcut on the desktop.*

10. *To create a shortcut on the toolbar, carry out the same process, but this time 'drop' the icon on the bottom toolbar to the right of existing icons.*

Activity 4.8   Using the print queue

1. *Open up a Word document. Click on the 'Print' icon.*

2. *Open up a second Word document. Click on 'File' from the pull-down menu. Select 'Print'.*

3. *To select any of the options listed, select 'Properties' from the print menu. To select the watermark 'Confidential', click on the 'Watermarks' tab. The text message will be defaulted to 'None'. Click on the arrow to scroll through the options to select 'Confidential'. Click on 'OK'.*

4. *To print two pages on one sheet, go to the 'Zoom' section of the print menu. Click on the arrow next to 'Pages per sheet' and alter from 'One page' to 'Two pages'. Click on 'OK'.*

5. *To print in landscape view, you need to go to 'Page Setup' from the 'File' menu. Click on 'Landscape' to change the page orientation and click on 'OK'. NB: You should alter the orientation of the page before selecting 'Print'.*

6. *To view the print queue, right-click on the printer icon that should have appeared on the toolbar at the bottom right side of the screen once you clicked on 'OK' to print. Click on 'Open all active Printers and Faxes'. You are now in the print queue.*

7. *You should see two documents in the queue. Select the first print job by highlighting it. Click on 'Printer' from the pull-down menu and select 'Pause Printing'.*

8. *Highlight the second document. Go to 'Document' in the pull-down menu and select 'Restart'.*

9. *Highlight the first document, go to 'Document' and click on 'Cancel'. You will be asked if you wish to cancel the selected print jobs. Click on 'Yes' and then close the print queue by clicking on X.*

Activity 5.1   Word processing and using shortcut keys

1. *Open Word by clicking on the relevant icon. You will be taken to a blank document called 'Document1'. Go to 'File' and select 'Save As'. Type in the name 'Initial Learning Profile' and save in your IT Skills folder.*

2. *Type in the information as set out in the activity. To create italicised letters, highlight the sentence by moving your cursor to the beginning of the sentence, depressing the left mouse key and then moving the cursor to the end of the sentence. Release the mouse key and then select the italicised I on the toolbar. Click again to start typing again, but you will need to re-click on the I icon first, otherwise all of the following text will be italicised.*

3. *To highlight or select text without using the mouse, position the cursor at the beginning of the text. NB: Make sure that you don't have either CAPS or NUM Lock on. Hold down the 'Shift' key and then use the keypad arrows to move to the end of the document. Once all of the document is highlighted, release the keys and then click on the 'justify' icon in the toolbar. This looks like a number of lines with both margins being equally aligned (if you aren't sure which is the right icon, just hover your mouse over it until you find the one that flashes up a box saying 'justify').*

4. *To create a border around the text, highlight the paragraph and then go to the toolbar and click on the icon that resembles a square with two dividing lines in it. This is usually to the right-hand side of the toolbar and will reveal 'Outside Border' if you hover your mouse over it.*

5. *To find individual words or phrases, hold down 'Ctrl' and 'F'. This will pop-up a box. In the 'Find What' box, type 'social work'. Then click on the 'Replace' Tab and type 'social care' in the 'Replace With' box. Then click on either 'Replace' or 'Replace All'. Close the box by clicking on X.*

6. *To delete words using shortcut keys, highlight the relevant word, then use 'Ctrl' and 'X' to delete it.*

7. *Re-save the document by clicking on the 'Save' icon. Click on the 'Print' icon.*

Activity 5.2   Clip art

1. *Open Word by double-clicking on the icon. You should now be taken to a blank 'Document1'.*

2. *To insert clip art, click on the 'Insert' pull-down menu (Figure A.3), then 'Picture' and then 'ClipArt'. Alternatively, if it is revealed, you can use the bottom toolbar shortcut, which is a framed person's head.*

Figure A.3

3. *ClipArt will then ask you for a category to search. Type 'Computer' in the 'Search for' box (or any other category you think relevant). Click on 'Search' and a number of hopefully suitable images will appear. Click on the one that you wish to use and it will then appear in your document in the position where your cursor had been flashing. Close 'ClipArt' by clicking on the X in the top right-hand corner.*

4. To manipulate the ClipArt image, click once on it. The 'Picture' toolbar will then appear. To resize the picture, click on the 'Format Picture' icon – this looks like a can of paint being poured. You will then see the pop-up 'Format Picture' box. Click on the 'Size' tab and using the toggle keys alter the size.

5. To centre the picture in the page, click on the 'Centre' icon as you would for text. To move the picture to a different place on the screen, make sure that it is highlighted. Then 'cut' it by clicking on the 'Cut' icon. Move your cursor to where you wish the image to be placed. Then click on the 'Paste' icon.

6. In order to utilise WordArt, you can either access it via the same route as above, or by clicking on the toolbar shortcut, which is a picture of an 'A' at an angle. Select a WordArt style from the Gallery by simply clicking on it to highlight it and then clicking on 'OK'. A pop-up 'Edit WordArt Text' box will then appear. Type directly into here, altering the font style and size if required. Click on 'OK' and it will appear in your Word document. Move it around as per previous step.

7. Save by clicking on the 'Save' icon and print out using the 'Print' icon.

Activity 5.3 — Mail merge

1. Open up a blank Word document. Go to 'File' and 'Save As' 'Carers Group Invite' in your IT Skills folder. Create a letterhead using WordArt as described above. Type in the letter given.

2. Then select 'Tools' from the menu system, then 'Letters and Mailings' and then 'Mail Merge Wizard'. In the right-hand pane a Wizard will appear.

3. Under 'Select Document Type' select 'Letters' and then click on 'Next'. Then click on 'Use Current Document' and then 'Next: Select Recipients'. This will allow you to create your data source, i.e. list of names that you want to be added into the template letter.

4. Click on 'Type a new list' and then click on 'Create'. A pop-up box will appear. Click on 'Customise', as you do not want all of the data categories on offer. Delete the categories that you do not want by highlighting them and then clicking on 'Delete'. A warning message will appear. Click on 'Yes'. Then add two new categories ('Name of cared for' and 'Social worker') by clicking on 'Add'. After each one click on 'OK'.

5. A 'New Address List' form will appear for you to enter your details into. Use the 'Tab' or 'Enter' key to move between fields. Click on 'New Entry' to add new records. When you have finished, click on 'Close'.

6. You will then see that you have created a mini database and need to save it. Call it 'Potential Group Members' and click on 'Save'.

7. Now click on 'Next: Write your letter'. Move your cursor to the gap in the letter that needs a First Name entered. Click on 'More Items' in the Wizard. Make sure that 'First Name' is highlighted, click on 'Insert'. Then click on 'Close'. Repeat for all the other gaps in your letter inserting the relevant field from the datasource.

8. Click on 'Next: Preview your letter'. Make sure that you have included spaces between 'First Name' and 'Last Name'. If they run into each other, go back one step and add a space.

9. Click on 'Next: Complete the Merge'. Click on 'Print' and the 'Merge to Print' pop-up box will appear. Select record no 3 (Jay Sidhu's) by typing 3 into the 'From' box. Click on 'OK' and the 'Print' pop-up box will appear. Click on 'OK'. The result will be as in Figure A.4.

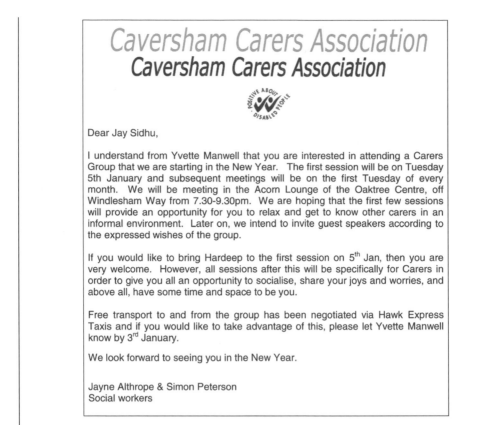

Caversham Carers Association
Caversham Carers Association

Dear Jay Sidhu,

I understand from Yvette Manwell that you are interested in attending a Carers Group that we are starting in the New Year. The first session will be on Tuesday 5th January and subsequent meetings will be on the first Tuesday of every month. We will be meeting in the Acorn Lounge of the Oaktree Centre, off Windlesham Way from 7.30-9.30pm. We are hoping that the first few sessions will provide an opportunity for you to relax and get to know other carers in an informal environment. Later on, we intend to invite guest speakers according to the expressed wishes of the group.

If you would like to bring Hardeep to the first session on 5th Jan, then you are very welcome. However, all sessions after this will be specifically for Carers in order to give you all an opportunity to socialise, share your joys and worries, and above all, have some time and space to be you.

Free transport to and from the group has been negotiated via Hawk Express Taxis and if you would like to take advantage of this, please let Yvette Manwell know by 3rd January.

We look forward to seeing you in the New Year.

Jayne Althrope & Simon Peterson
Social workers

Figure A.4

Activity 5.4 Using a template

1. Open Word. Go to 'File' and select 'New'.

2. You will then need to select a 'General Template'. A template pop-up box should then appear.

3. Select 'Other Documents' from the options on offer in the toolbar. Click on 'Resume Wizard', then 'OK' and follow the step-by-step instructions.

4. When you have created all of the headings, click on 'Finish'. Your CV will then be created using some of your Personal Details already entered.

5. To enter more information into the CV, click on the [Click here and enter information] and then start typing. The default text will then disappear.

6. To change the font of the CV, highlight the whole document. Then click on the arrow next to the 'Font bar' e.g. the font bar below contains the font 'Garamond' (see Figure A.5). By clicking on the arrow, you can scroll through alternative font options.

Figure A.5

7. Click on 'File' then select 'Save As'. Save your CV in your IT Skills folder.

| Activity *5.5* | *Spell checker* |

1. *Open Word and go to 'File'. Select 'Save As' and save the document as 'A Harsh Form of Justice' in your IT Skills folder.*

2. *Type in the article and when you have finished this, highlight the entire document. As described above, alter the font using the font bar.*

3. *With the text still highlighted, click on the 'Justify' icon on the toolbar. This will make sure that both margins are equally aligned.*

4. *Keep the text highlighted and go to 'Format' from the pull-down menu. Select 'Paragraph'. Under the heading 'Spacing', you will see an option box for 'Line Spacing'. Click on the arrow next to it and you should be able to select 'Double'. Click on 'OK'.*

5. *To use the spell-checker, you can either highlight the entire document, or move the cursor to the beginning of the document. Click on the 'ABC' icon on the toolbar. The Spelling and Grammar pop-up box will appear and will highlight every word that the computer believes is misspelled (Figure A.6)*

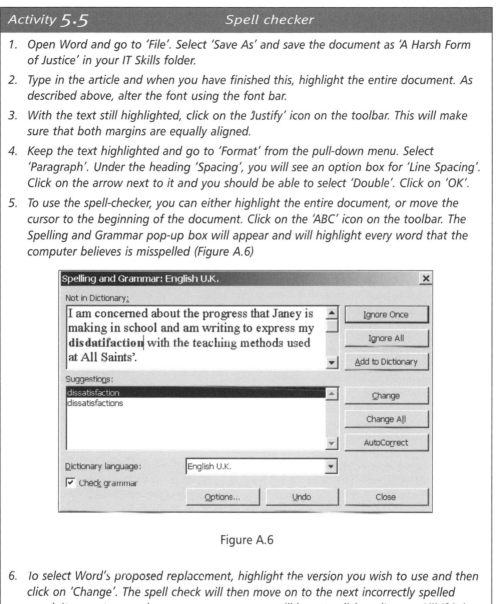

Figure A.6

6. *To select Word's proposed replacement, highlight the version you wish to use and then click on 'Change'. The spell check will then move on to the next incorrectly spelled word. It cannot recognise proper nouns so you will have to click on 'Ignore All' if it is a person's name or an acronym such as ASBO that you have used.*

7. *To create a footer, click on 'View' from the pull-down menu. Select 'Header and Footer'. You will then see a dashed line appear at the bottom and top of your page as well as the Header/Footer toolbar. Scroll down to the bottom of your page in order to add details into the footer.*

8. *Place the cursor in the footer box and then click on 'Insert AutoText'. Select 'Filename and Path' and then 'Page X of Y'. You can centre these within the footer if you wish by using the text alignment icons on the toolbar.*

9. *Click on 'Close' and then 'Save'.*

Activity 5.6 — Inserting pictorial characters/symbols

1. Open up a Word document.

2. Go to the pull-down menu 'Insert' and select 'Symbol'. Figure A.7 shows the box that will appear and there are a variety of options that you can select from scrolling through each of the 'font' sections. Webdings and Wingdings have plenty of symbols to choose from.

3. Click on 'Insert' once you have highlighted the symbol that you wish to use. This will automatically insert the symbol into your document. Click on 'Close' or X to close the box.

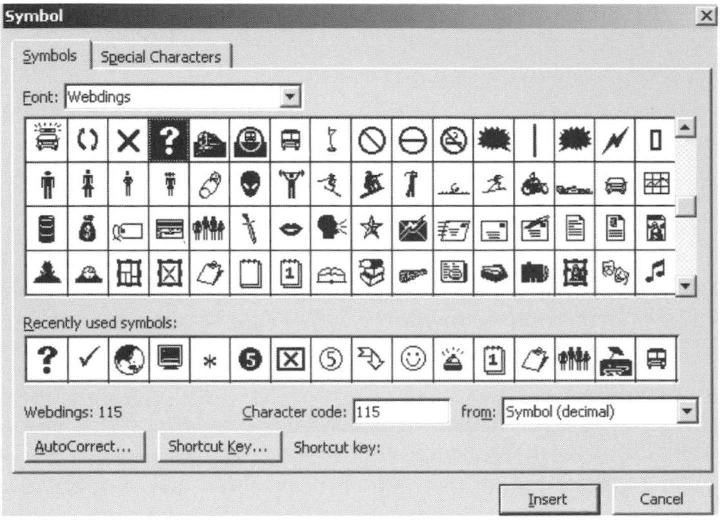

Figure A.7

4. Save in your IT Skills folder by going to the 'File' pull-down menu and selecting 'Save As' Call the poster by an appropriate file name and then click on 'Save'.

Activity 5.7 — Creating/inserting a table

1. Open Word and create a new document.

2. Go to the 'Table' menu and select 'Insert Table'. If you have clicked on the icon, you will only be able to create a table that is a maximum of 5 x 4 cells, which is not large enough for this activity.

3. You will then be asked for the number of rows and columns.

4. In order to apply a format or style to the table, highlight the entire table and then right-click with the cursor over the table. Select 'Table Autoformat' and you will then be offered a range of different styles to apply to the table. The format that is used in the Workbook is 'Table Contemporary'.

5. Click on 'Apply'.

6. Save in your IT Skills folder and print out a copy by clicking on the 'Print' icon.

Activity 5.8   *Inserting an organisation chart*

1. *Open Word by double-clicking on the icon.*
2. *The Organisation Chart is available via the 'Insert' toolbar. Select 'Picture' and then 'Organisation Chart'. The following template (Figure A.8) will appear along with a menu bar.*

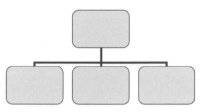

Figure A.8

3. *By clicking in each of the boxes you can add any text. When the box is highlighted, you can also then add connecting boxes on either the side or below. The menu bar will offer you a number of different options to add when you click on 'Insert Shaper' in the form of 'Co-workers', 'Subordinates' or 'Assistants'.*
4. *If the box is too small for your text/your text too large for the box, you can highlight the text and change it using the usual font options. You can also add pictures to the boxes.*
5. *Save your chart by going to 'File' and selecting 'Save As ...'. Choose an appropriate name for your document and ensure that it is saved in your IT Skills folder.*

Activity 6.1   *Creating a spreadsheet*

1. *Open Excel by double-clicking on the icon.*
2. *Enter the data into the blank spreadsheet. Use the arrow keys to move from one row to the next. Pressing the 'Enter' key will also move the cursor down the screen. If you wish to move across the screen from column to column, you can press the 'Tab' key. Alternatively you can click on the relevant cell with your mouse.*
3. *When you have entered all of your data, you may notice that the columns are not wide enough to display all of the text. Move your cursor to the line that separates the columns in the grey header row and you should see that it changes from a cross to an arrow bisecting a line. Double-click and the columns should automatically re-size.*
4. *Type the title at the bottom of the data. Save your spreadsheet in your IT Skills folder by going to 'File' and selecting 'Save As...'.*
5. *Highlight all of your data by clicking and dragging with the mouse. Then right click with the mouse to reveal the pull-down menu and select 'Copy'. You will then see a moving dotted line around the edge of your highlighted text.*
6. *Open either Word or PowerPoint and select where you would like the table to be placed; e.g. move the cursor to the right place in a Word document or find a blank slide in PowerPoint presentation. Right-click with the mouse again and select 'Paste'.*
7. *Click on the 'Print' icon.*

Activity 6.2 Reading and printing out an existing spreadsheet

1. *Open Excel by double-clicking on the icon. Go to 'File' and 'Open' and open up your previously created spreadsheet.*

2. *To hide columns, highlight them by clicking on the column header, e.g. D, then select 'Format' from the pull-down menus, then 'Column', then 'Hide'. (To reveal hidden columns later, highlight the columns on either side, e.g. C and E and then go to 'Format', 'Column' and 'Unhide'.)*

3. *Open Internet Explorer and type in the web address given in the previous activity. Either print a copy of the information needed or write it down to add to your spreadsheet.*

4. *Return to Excel and type the information directly into two columns at the far right of your spreadsheet.*

5. *To print only the view that is seen on the screen, highlight your table and then select the 'File' menu, 'Print Area' and then 'Set Print Area'. To print out the spreadsheet in landscape view, go to 'File' and select 'Page Setup'. Make sure that the button next to 'Landscape' is highlighted. Click on 'OK'. Click on the 'Print' icon.*

6. *To save the amended spreadsheet, go to 'File' and select 'Save As...'. Save it by a slightly different name to the original one so that you can identify the changes that you have made.*

Activity 6.3 Formatting a spreadsheet

1. *Open Excel and your spreadsheet 'Unicef Demographic Comparisons' as above.*

2. *Highlight all of the cells in the heading row, i.e. row 1, by clicking on the greyed out header 1 with your mouse.*

3. *To alter the font, use the font option in the toolbar at the top of the screen.*

4. *Repeat with the first column, i.e. column A.*

5. *To change the background colour, highlight all of the cells and then right-click with the mouse. This will reveal a pop-up menu. Select 'Format Cells' then 'Patterns'. Choose a colour by clicking directly on it, then click on 'OK'.*

6. *To create a border, highlight all of the cells and right-click with the mouse. Select 'Border' from the pop-up menu , as in Figure A.9*

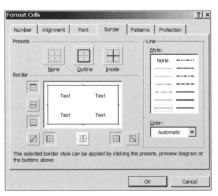

Figure A.9

7. *Click on the 'Outline' box icon under 'Presets' and then click on the middle box icon in the 'Border' section. This will ensure that only vertical lines are dashed within your table. Click on 'OK'.*

8. *Go to 'File' and 'Save As'. Use a different name for the amended table and save in your IT Skills folder. Select the 'Print' icon to print a copy.*

Activity 6.4 — Creating pie/column charts

1. *Open Excel by double-clicking on the icon. Enter in the data provided.*

2. *For the pie chart, you will need to hide the columns containing data other than the field labels and Wycombe percentages. To hide the columns, first highlight them and then right-click to reveal the pop-up menu. Select 'Hide'.*

3. *In order to create a pie chart of the remaining data you can either click on the 'Chart' icon on the toolbar which will take you to the Chart Wizard, or you can go to the 'Insert' menu and select 'Chart' there.*

4. *The Chart Wizard will first ask you to select what type of chart you wish to create. Select 'Pie' by highlighting it and a preview of sub-types will appear in the box. Select one of them and click on 'Next'.*

5. *The data range will then be requested. Using your mouse, highlight the remaining two visible columns in your spreadsheet. Then click on 'Next'.*

6. *Next, the Wizard will ask you to create a title for the chart by entering it directly into the box. By selecting 'Legend' you can create a key, by selecting 'Data Labels' you can create arrows to the pie segments including percentages, etc. Click on 'Next'.*

7. *You will then be asked if you wish to save this chart on a separate work sheet, or have it embedded within the work sheet that you are currently working on. Select one of the options and then click on 'Finish'.*

8. *Follow the same process to create a column chart, but this time, you need to reveal all of the columns. To 'unhide' columns you need to highlight the columns on either side of where the column should be i.e. if you have hidden column B, you need to highlight columns A and C. Then go to 'Format' from the pull-down menu, then 'Column' and then 'Unhide'.*

9. *Save by clicking on the 'Save' icon.*

10. *To copy charts into Word, right-click on them with the mouse to reveal a pop-up menu. Select 'Copy'.*

11. *Open Word by double-clicking on the icon. Click on the 'Paste' icon and your chart will be copied into the Word document.*

12. *Save both the spreadsheet with the charts in it and your new Word document in your IT Skills folder by going to 'File' and selecting 'Save As...'.*

13. *Print by clicking on the 'Print' icon.*

Activity 6.5 — Ordering data alphabetically

1. *Open Excel by double-clicking on the icon.*

2. *In order to order names alphabetically, you will need to highlight the entire spreadsheet, not just the column including the names. If you only highlight the column*

including the names, the data in the other columns will not marry up any more.

3. *Click on either the menu bar 'Data', then 'Sort', or the toolbar icon 'A-Z'. This will automatically sort the data alphabetically.*

4. *To then further sort the data by minimum age, highlight all of the data again, select 'Data' on the menu bar, then 'Sort' and you will then be asked to select with which category you would like to sort the data. Select 'Minimum Age', leave the bullet highlighted and click 'OK' (Figure A.10).*

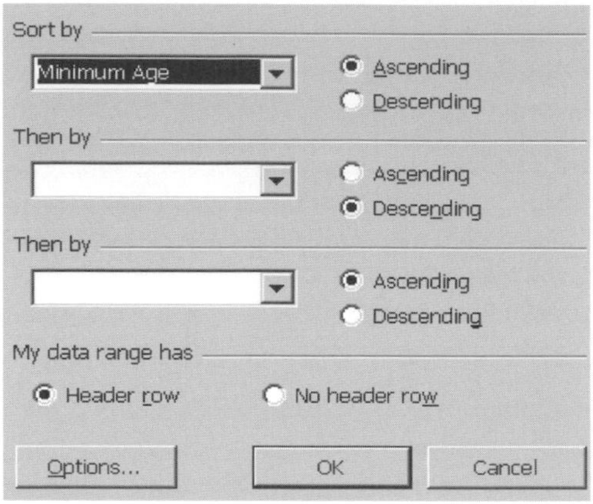

Figure A.10

Activity 6.6   *Using the SUM formula*

1. *Open Excel by double-clicking on the icon.*

2. *Create a new spreadsheet and 'Save As...' 'Income/Expenditure' in your IT Skills folder.*

3. *Type directly into the cells by positioning the cursor over the cell into which you wish to add data.*

4. *In order to create a SUM formula, highlight all of the cells that you wish to add up in any one of your columns, making sure that you include the cell that is 'TOTAL'.*

5. *Click on the Greek symbol Σ in the toolbar. This will automatically total all of your figures. If you then highlight your 'TOTAL' cell, you will now note that the formula =SUM(C3:C18) has appeared in the formula bar. Instead of doing the above steps 4 and 5, you could have entered this formula directly into the formula bar for the 'TOTAL' cell and the outcome would be the same.*

6. *In order to create a subtraction formula, you need to write a formula for the 'TOTAL AMOUNT LEFT' cell. Write this directly in the formula bar using the cell co-ordinates for the 'TOTAL' cells. Your formula should read something like =(B28-E28). Once entered, click on the green ✔ and Excel will perform the subtraction calculation.*

Activity 6.7   *Creating and moving between data sheets*

1. *Open Excel by double-clicking on the icon.*

2. *Go to 'File' and 'Save As' and save your new spreadsheet in your IT Skills folder.*

3. *To create separate worksheets, move to the tabs at the bottom of the spreadsheet that*

are defaulted to <Sheet1> <Sheet2> <Sheet3>. Right-hand click on <Sheet1> to reveal a pop-up menu. Select 'Rename' and then type 'January' over the existing name. Repeat with the next two sheets.

4. To create additional worksheets, go to 'Insert' from the pull-down menu. Select 'Worksheet'. Repeat a further 8 times so that you have a worksheet for each month of the year.

5. You will now find that 'March' is at the end of the list of worksheets (which you need to rename as per step 3). To move it back to its correct chronological position, hold down the left mouse button over it. You will see a 'Sheet of Paper' icon appear along with an arrow head. Drag the sheet back to its correct position and then release the mouse button.

6. In order to commence working on January's worksheet, simply click on the 'January' tab. Enter in the list of details following the format exemplified in the question.

7. To copy these details across into the following worksheets, highlight all of the information entered by positioning the cursor in the top-left cell you wish to highlight, holding down the left mouse button and then dragging the mouse to highlight all of the cells required. Either right-click to reveal a pop-up menu and select 'Copy' or click on the 'Copy' icon from the toolbar. Click on February's worksheet and move the cursor to the A1 box. Click on the 'Paste' icon in the toolbar. Repeat for the remaining worksheets.

8. Type the information requested into each worksheet.

9. To alter the format of the header columns, highlight the row and then right-click with the mouse. Select 'Format Cells' and then choose an option. If you wish to change the background colour, select 'Patterns'. In order to italicise the clients' names highlight the relevant column. Either select the 'Italics' icon from the toolbar, or right click in order to bring up the pop-up menu and select 'Format Cells' and then 'Font'.

10. To copy the formatting across the worksheets, highlight the relevant cells and then click on the 'Copy' icon in the toolbar. Move to the next worksheet by clicking on the relevant tab. Highlight the cells that you wish to apply the formatting to. Right click with the mouse and a pop-up menu will appear. Select 'Paste Special' and then click on the button next to 'Formats'. Click on 'OK'.

11. Repeat for each subsequent worksheet.

12. Save by clicking on the 'Save' icon.

Activity 6.8　　　　　*Using the COUNTIF formula*

1. Open up Excel by double-clicking on the icon.

2. Go to 'File' from the pull-down menu and click on 'Open'. Select your parenting group spreadsheet.

3. Create a new column F for 'Total Attendance'.

4. You now need to create a formula. Highlight cell F3 which should relate to your first client. Click on the 'fx' icon next to the formula bar. You will then see a pop-up 'Insert Function' menu box appear. Scroll through 'All' categories to find 'COUNTIF'. Click on it to select it and then click on 'OK'.

5. A 'Functions Arguments' pop-up box will then appear. You can either directly type in your range, e.g. B3:E3, or use your cursor to highlight the relevant cells in the

spreadsheet. In the 'Criteria' box type 'Yes'. Click on 'OK'. You will now see the formula: =COUNTIF(B3:E3, ''Yes''). The number of 'Yes' responses should have been tallied and appear in F3.

6. To copy the formula across into the cells below, highlight the cell F3. Click on the 'Copy' icon from the toolbar. Then highlight the cells that also require the COUNTIF formula, e.g. F4, F5, F6, etc. Right click with the mouse and select 'Paste Special'. Click on the button next to 'Formulas'.

7. To copy the formula across to the other worksheets, click on the 'February' worksheet tab. Highlight the column that you wish to copy the formula into. Right click with the mouse and select 'Paste Special' and select 'Formula' again. Repeat with the other worksheets.

8. Create a header in Column G titled 'Total Attendance over Duration of Group'.

9. Highlight cell G3. Click on the 'Σ' icon from the toolbar. This will automatically start a SUM formula in the formula bar and should read: =SUM( ). A cell reference will appear between the brackets according to which cell in the spreadsheet is contained within the flashing highlighted box.

10. Move the highlighted cell to F3 by clicking on F3. Your formula should now read: =SUM(F3). Type in a comma after F3, i.e. =SUM(F3,).

11. Now click on the February worksheet. Highlight F3 on this worksheet and your formula in the bar should now read: =SUM(F3,February!F3). Insert another comma after the second F3. Repeat for all of the worksheets up until and including June. Do not include a comma after June.

12. Return to January's worksheet. Your formula bar should look like the one shown in Figure A.11 and all of the figures in the G column should be the sum of each client's total attendance over the six-month period.

	G3	▼	*f*ₓ	=SUM(January!F3,February!F3,March!F3,April!F3,May!F3,June!F3)		
	A	B	C	D	E	F	G
1	Client Name	Date of Session				Total Attendance	Total Attendance over
2		03/01/2005	10/01/2005	17/01/2005	25/01/2005		Course of Group
3	Jayne Tomlins	Yes	Yes	Yes	Yes	4	4
4	Frank Tomlins	No	No	No	No	0	5
5	Serena Fachey	Yes	Yes	Yes	Yes	4	24
6	Tracey Dodd	Yes	No	No	No	1	6
7	Amity Jacobs	Yes	Yes	Yes	Yes	4	24
8	George Jacobs	No	Yes	Yes	Yes	3	14
9	Christine O'Donohue	Yes	No	Yes	Yes	3	18
10	Simone Tyree	No	Yes	Yes	Yes	3	18
11	Jamie Hathaway	Yes	Yes	Yes	Yes	4	24
12	Fariah Constantine	Yes	Yes	Yes	Yes	4	24
13	Precious Oleywole	Yes	Yes	Yes	Yes	4	24
14	Amy Lovelace	No	No	No	No	0	0
15	Zoe Prestwick	Yes	Yes	No	Yes	3	18

Figure A.11

13. Click on 'Save' and remaining in January's worksheet click on the 'Print' icon.

Activity 7.1   *Creating a database using Access*

1. *Open Access by double-clicking on the icon.*

2. *Click on 'Blank Database' and then you will then see a pop-up box asking you to save your Database before you start working on it (in contrast to other applications that allow you to create files before saving). Save the database under the name 'Client Contact Details' in your IT Skills folder.*

3. *You will then be taken to the main view of Access and in order to start creating a table in the design view, you need to double-click on that option offered in the pop-up menu. A blank sheet will then appear with the cursor flashing in the column entitled 'Field Name'.*

4. *Type in the first field that you wish to create: 'Name' and then either press 'Tab' or 'Return' to take you to the 'Data Type' column. You will notice that a little arrow has appeared on the right-hand side of the box. If you click on this a pull-down menu will appear and you can select your data type by double-clicking on the highlighted option. Use 'Tab' or 'Return' to move to the next field.*

5. *After you have filled in all of your fields and data types, click on the 'Save' icon in the toolbar. A prompt will appear asking the name of the table. Save as 'Keyworker Contact Details'.*

6. *You will then return to the main screen of the database and should now see your newly created table identified in the box. If you double-click on your table you will see a form has been created in order for you to enter your data into the table, as in Figure A.12.*

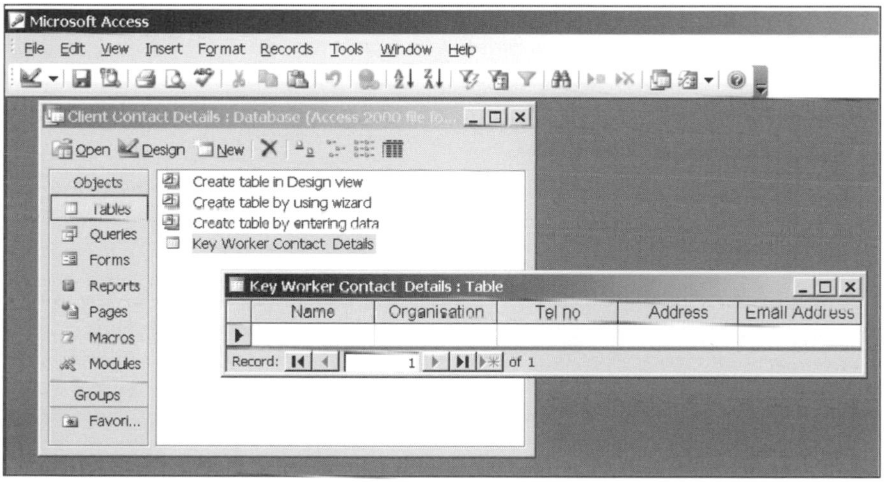

Figure A.12

7. *You can now start entering your data directly into this form, pressing the 'Tab' key to move across the fields. Once you have filled in all of the boxes, press 'Enter' to start the next record.*

8. *Once you have entered all of the records, click on the 'Save' icon in the toolbar. Then click on the 'X' in the top right-hand corner of the form window in order to close it and return to the main screen.*

9. Double-click on 'Key Worker Contact Details' now and you will find all of your records in a datasheet. To sort them alphabetically by organisation, highlight the 'Organisation' column by clicking on it. You can then either sort the list by clicking on the sort 'A-Z' icon on the toolbar, or by selecting 'Sort' from the 'Records' menu and then 'Sort Ascending'.

10. In order to print your records in landscape view, you need to remain in the datasheet view. Go to 'File' and select 'Page Set-up'. Click on the 'Page' tab and then click on the 'Landscape' button followed by 'OK'.

11. To ensure that you are able to see the full details of each field, move your cursor within the datasheet to the grey header bar. If you position the cursor on the line separating two field names you will see that it changes to a thick line cross-sected with an arrow. Once this happens, double-click with your mouse and the column to the left will automatically resize to allow all of the text to be seen.

12. Once you have re-formatted the table, click on the 'Save' icon and then 'Print'.

Activity 7.2 — Opening an existing database using Access

1. Double-click on the Access icon and select the 'Client Contact Details' database. You may see a warning that the file may not be safe. However, as you created the file, you can safely click on 'Open'.

2. Double-click on the highlighted 'Key Worker Contact Details' table. Go to the 'View' pulldown menu and select 'Design View'.

3. To set the Primary Key, select the 'Client Name' row by moving the cursor to it. Click on the key icon on the toolbar. You will now see a key next to the row, as in Figure A.13.

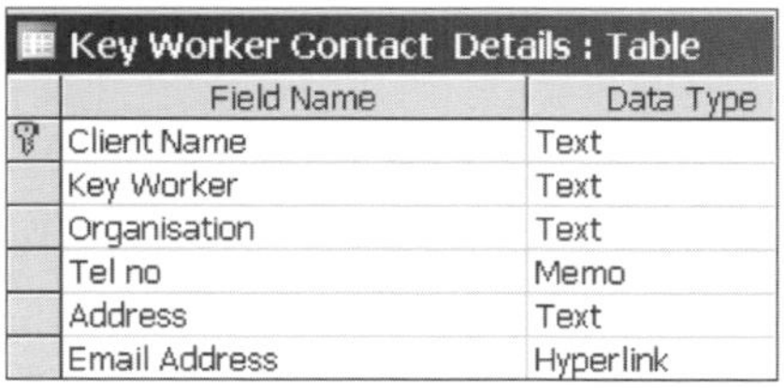

Field Name	Data Type
Client Name	Text
Key Worker	Text
Organisation	Text
Tel no	Memo
Address	Text
Email Address	Hyperlink

Key Worker Contact Details : Table

Figure A.13

Alternatively you can go to the 'File' pull-down menu and select 'Primary Key' from here.

4. To create a form, close down your datasheet (not the program) and click on the 'Form' option on the left-hand side of the main box in Access and then select the Form Wizard. Alternatively, you can select 'Form' from the 'Insert' pull-down menu and select the Form Wizard from there. Follow the instructions and once you have clicked on 'Finish' you should see a form appear with your first record already on display.

5. Click on the ▶* tab to progress to the last record and then enter your four new records. Click on 'Save' when you have finished. Stay in the 'Form' view.

6. In order to sort the records alphabetically, click on the 'A-Z' icon in the toolbar.

7. There are many ways to filter the records so that only the Chaucer Day Centre records are revealed. One way is to go to the 'Records' pull-down menu, select 'Filter' and then 'Filter by Form'. You will then see a blank form and by moving your cursor to highlight

the 'Organisation Box' you will get a pull-down menu option from which you can select Chaucer Day Centre, as in Figure A.14.

Key Worker Contact Details: Filter by Form	_ □ ×
Client Name	
Key Worker	
Organisation	"Chaucer Day Centre" ▼
Tel no	Canterbury Carers Chaucer Day Centre Community Mental Health Team
Address	District Nurse Fastnet Home Alarms FSG Homecare
Email Address	Help the Aged Reliance Homecare
Look for / Or /	

Figure A.14

8. To print all the records, go to the 'File' menu and select 'Print'. All twelve of your records will then be printed out in the form format.

Activity 7.3   Exporting an existing database to Excel

1. Open Access and your database 'Client Contact Details'.

2. Go to 'File' and then select 'Export'. This will reveal a pop-up menu which will save your database so that it can be exported to Excel. Make sure that you save the database in your IT Skills Folder as an Excel 97-2002 file (the default option is a .mdb file).

3. Click on 'Export'.

4. Now open Excel and check to see that you are able to open your database as a spreadsheet file by going to 'File' and then 'Open'.

5. Your data should then appear in spreadsheet format, but you will not be able to see all of the details. To resize the columns, move the cursor to the column header row and hover it over the line that separates the columns. It will then change to a crossed arrow. Then double-click and the column will automatically resize.

6. When you are happy with the format, go to the 'File' menu again and select 'Page Setup'. This will allow you to print the spreadsheet in landscape format if you click on the 'Landscape' button. Click on 'OK'.

7. Return to the 'File' menu and select 'Print' or click on the print icon on the toolbar.

Activity 7.4   Creating a relational database using Access

1. Open Access and your database 'Contact Details'.

2. To create a new table, make sure that you are in the table object view and then click on 'New'. Select 'Datasheet View'.

3. A new datasheet will then appear for you to add your data to. Rather than typing in each client's name individually, you might like to copy them across from your original table. To do this, go to your original table in datasheet view and highlight the entire column of client names by clicking on the header row. Then right-click and select

'Copy'. Go to the Datasheet view of your new table and in the first column, right-click and select 'Paste'.

4. Go to the 'Design View' and rename the column 'Client name' and then proceed as per the previous activity to create the field names, data types and primary key for your new forms.

5. Return to the 'Datasheet' view to add the rest of your data.

6. Save the table by clicking on the 'Save' icon in the toolbar. A pop-up menu will appear asking you to 'Save as' with a default option of 'Table1'. Rename the table 'Client Contact Details' and click on 'OK'.

7. Repeat the above for the table 'Family Contact Details'.

8. Your database should now have three tables appearing in the box.

9. Go to the pull-down menu 'Tools' and select 'Relationships'. A pop-up menu will appear with one of your tables highlighted within it. Click on 'Add'. Then highlight the other two tables in turn, clicking on 'Add' each time. Then click on 'Close'

10. You will then see your three tables on the screen, and you can resize the boxes by clicking and dragging on the bottom right corner of the box so that you can see all of the text. The 'Client Name' should appear in bold in each table to indicate that it is the Primary Key.

11. To create relationships between the tables, move your cursor to 'Client Name' in the 'Client Contact Details' table. Click and drag from here to the 'Client Name' in the 'Key Worker Contact Details'. A box will then appear, as shown in Figure A.15.

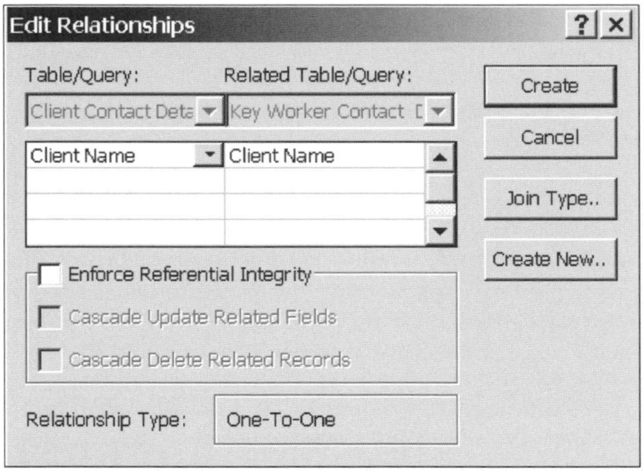

Figure A.15

12. Check the box that asks if you wish to 'Enforce Referential Integrity' and then click on 'Create'. You will then see a line appear joining the two records.

13. Repeat step 8 again with 'Family Contact Details' to 'Client Contact Details'. You have now created your 'Relationships' between the tables which will allow all three of the tables to be searched at the same time.

14. To print your 'Relationships', go to the 'File' pull-down menu and select 'Print Relationships'. You will then see a Print preview screen of your relationships. Right-click to reveal a pop-up menu and select 'Print' from here.

Activity 7.5   *Carrying out a search in Access*

1. Open Access and your database 'Client Contact Details'.

2. Click on 'Queries' in the database window. Select 'Create Query Using a Wizard'. A pop-up box will then appear asking which fields you would like in your table. If you click on the pull-down menu tab next to the Tables/Queries bar, you should be able to choose from the three tables that you have already created.

3. Select 'Table: Client Contact Details' and then highlight the field 'Client Name' in the box below and click on the > button. The field 'Client Name' will then move from the left to the right box.

4. Select 'Table: Key Worker Contact Details' and then highlight the field 'Key Worker' and click on the > button.

5. Select 'Table: Family Contact Details' and then highlight the field 'Contact Name' and click on the > button. Repeat for 'Tel no'. If you select any field in error, simply click on the < and your selection will be undone.

6. When all the relevant fields have been selected, click on 'Next'. You will then be required to give a name for your query. Click on 'Next'. Your query will then run and you will see a datasheet with the four fields and data from all of them revealed.

7. For the query relating to the clients who attend the Chaucer Day Centre, carry out steps 2–7 but select all of the fields (remember that you only need to highlight 'Client Name' once) from all of the tables.

8. When the Wizard invites you to open or modify your query, this time you need to modify it so click on 'Modify the Query Design' and then click on 'Finish'.

9. You will then see the design view for your query. Locate the column that relates to 'Organisation' – this may be off the screen, so you may need to scroll across to it. In the row 'Criteria', type ''Chaucer Day Centre'' (including the speech marks), as in Figure A.16.

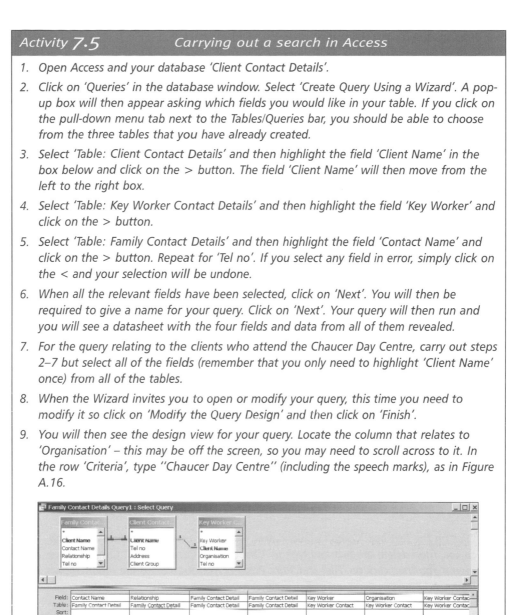

Figure A.16

10. Click on 'Save' and then the red exclamation mark in the toolbar. This will run your query and you should see three records appearing in the datasheet.

11. To print out these records without running a report, go to 'File' and select 'Page Setup'. Select 'Landscape'. Then click on 'OK' and then 'Print'. Your three records will then print out. However, they will spread over two pages and will therefore not be in a very user-friendly format.

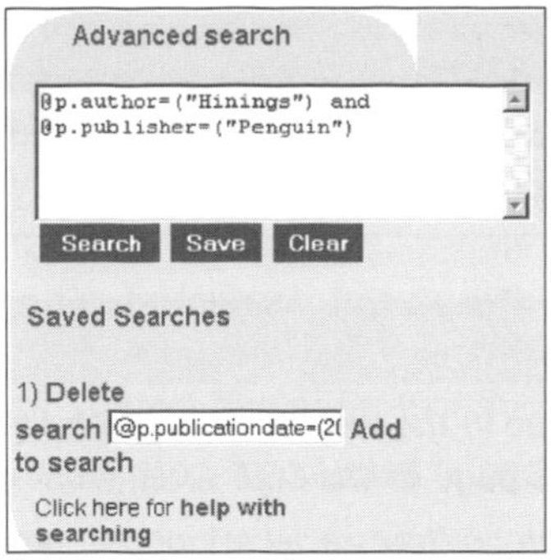

Figure A.20

11. *Highlight the 'Field Tag' for author and click once on this. Be patient, as it will then appear in the large box, but you will need to scroll up the screen in order to see that it has happened. Then type 'Hinings' between the speech marks. Do the same for the 'Field Tag' for publisher. Then click on 'Search'. At the time of writing you could find 1 record.*

12. *Follow the same procedure for 'Howe' and select the 'Field Tag' for publication date. At the time of writing you could find 3 records.*

13. *In order to search broadly for research journals or books relevant to the essay, return to the home page. Type a topic into the box under 'Browse Social Care Topics'. A good choice would be 'Race relations'. Click on 'Search'. You will then be taken to another page with a long list of topics. Scroll down until you find 'Race relations' highlighted in red. Click on this and you will be taken to all relevant articles and books relating to this topic.*

Activity 8.1 — *Preparing a new presentation*

1. *Open PowerPoint by double-clicking on the icon.*

2. *The first slide should be defaulted to a title slide with two text boxes, one with <Click to add title> and one with <Click to add subtitle>. Position your cursor in the first box and type in the title. Repeat for the subtitle.*

3. *Click on the icon for 'New Slide' on the toolbar or alternatively select 'New Slide' from the 'Insert' pull-down menu. Type your heading into the main part of the slide and then repeat this step for the next five slides.*

4. *To delete the title text box from these slides, click within the title text box. Then move your cursor onto the border around the text box. Click on it with the mouse so that the border changes format to dots rather than diagonal lines. Then right click with the mouse so that a pop-up menu appears. Select 'Cut'. You should now be left with just the main body of the slide.*

5. *To alter the font, highlight the text by clicking and dragging with the mouse. Once the text is highlighted, select a different font option from the toolbar.*

6. *To insert WordArt behind the text, either click on the WordArt icon on the bottom toolbar, or go to the pull-down 'Insert' menu, select 'Picture' and then 'WordArt'.*

7. *Select a WordArt style by clicking on the style of your choice and then clicking on 'OK'.*

A pop-up 'Edit WordArt Text' box will then appear. Type in your number. You will need to ensure that the font size is quite large, e.g. 96, so that it fills the whole slide. Click on 'OK'.

8. *Your number will now appear on the slide, but will be obscuring pre-existing text. Right click with the mouse to reveal a pop-up menu and the WordArt toolbar. Select 'Order' and 'Send to back'. The number should then appear layered under your text.*

9. *Repeat for all six slides.*

10. *Open Internet Explorer and type the address into the address bar. Click on 'Go' or hit the Return key. Print the full details for each of the Expectations.*

11. *To add additional slides to the presentation in the relevant position, move your cursor to your slide titled 'Communication Skills and Information Sharing'. Go to 'Insert' from the pull-down menu and select 'New slide'. You will then be able to insert a blank slide in between the existing slides 2 and 3. Repeat step 4.*

12. *Enter in the information gathered from the TOPSS web pages, making sure that your slides do not look too cluttered. To create bullet points, click on the 'bullet point' or numbers icon on the toolbar. For example, if you look at the slides in Figure A.21, slides 10 and 11 would be easier to understand than slides 13 and 15.*

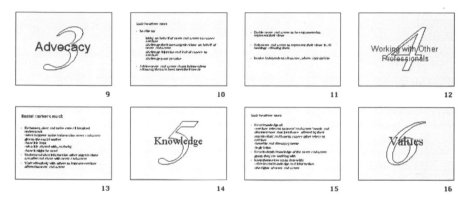

Figure A.21

13. *If you want to have letters a–l appearing rather than the default numbering system, click on 'Format' from the pull-down menu and then select 'Bullets and Numbering'. Select the format that you require by clicking on it and then clicking on 'OK'.*

14. *Create a final slide at the end. Go to 'File' and select 'Save As'. Save the presentation in your IT Skills folder.*

15. *To hide slides, go to the 'Slide Sorter' by clicking on the icon in the bottom left-hand side of the screen. Alternatively go to the 'View' pull-down menu and select 'Slide Sorter'.*

16. *Right click with the mouse on the slide that you wish to hide. This will reveal a pop-up menu. Select 'Hide Slide'. Alternatively, click on the 'Hide Slide' icon on the tool bar. You will then see that the number relating to the slide will appear in a box with the number crossed through. Repeat.*

17. *To view the amended show, click on 'Slideshow' from the pull-down menu. Select 'View Show' and press either 'Return' or click with the mouse to progress the slides.*

18. To print out the slides, go to 'Print' from the 'File' menu. The pop-up menu box should be defaulted to print slides. Click on 'OK'.

Activity 8.2 *Preparing a presentation using a design template*

1. Open PowerPoint by double-clicking on the icon. Go to 'File' and click on 'Save As...'. Type 'Key Legislation for Social Workers' into the 'File name' box and click on 'Save'.
2. To select a 'design template', either click on the 'Design' icon on the right-hand side of the toolbar or go to the pull-down menu 'Format' and select 'Slide Design'. Select a design from the pane on the right-hand side by simply clicking once on the image.
3. The title slide will then appear automatically. Enter the relevant information.
4. Click on 'New Slide' to create further slides and click on <Click to add title> in order to enter the title for the slide. Click on <Click to add text> to add bullet-pointed lines in the main body of the slide. By hitting 'Enter' after each line you can create a new bullet point.
5. To create a slide with a simple table in it, add a new slide with the standard format and then click on the 'Table' icon on the toolbar. Drag your cursor to highlight cells two wide by four deep. Click once with the mouse and a table will then appear in your slide. Alternatively, select 'Format' from the pull-down menu and then 'Slide Layout'. Click on the outline that represents a slide with a table and title.
6. Type the information directly into the table using the 'Tab' key to move between cells.
7. Click on 'New Slide' to create final slide.
8. Save by clicking on the 'Save' icon.

Activity 8.3 *Inserting other files into a presentation*

1. Open PowerPoint by double-clicking on the icon. Go to 'File' and 'Save As...' and save your presentation in your IT Skills folder.
2. Go to 'Format' and 'Slide Design' and select a Design template as described in the previous activity. Type in the information for the title slide as appropriate.
3. Click on 'New Slide' and type in the title. Repeat.
4. Open Internet Explorer and use a search engine or one of the websites given to find the relevant information to complete the slides.
5. Save the presentation by clicking on the 'Save' icon. Click on the 'Print' icon then close this presentation by clicking on the X at the far end of the toolbar, not the X on the window – this will close PowerPoint completely.
6. Open your previous presentation by clicking on the 'Open' icon on the toolbar and locating your presentation. Click on 'Open' once you have highlighted it.
7. Scroll through the slides until you reach the one on Older People. Go to the 'Insert' pull-down menu and select 'Slides from File'. You will then need to browse your drives in order to find your Carers presentation. Once you have located it, click on 'Open'. You will see that the individual slides from the presentation will appear in a preview pane. Click on the relevant slide that you wish to insert about Carers Legislation and click on 'Insert', then 'Close'.

8. *Alter the title of the slide by moving your cursor to the title and simply deleting the existing title and retyping the new one.*

9. *Save by clicking on the 'Save' icon.*

10. *To print out handouts, click on 'File', then 'Print'. In the bottom left side of the box, it shows 'Print what?' Select 'Handouts'. You then will have the option of deciding how many handouts per page, e.g. 6, 3, or 1. (Selecting '3' will give blank lines next to the slide.)*

11. *Click on 'OK'.*

Activity 8.4   Altering an existing presentation

1. *Double-click on the PowerPoint icon to open it. Go to 'File' and click on 'Open' and select the relevant presentation.*

2. *To alter the title slide you can either click on the main slide showing, or on the Outline view on the left-hand side of the screen. Simply overtype, or delete the text that is no longer required and enter the revised text.*

3. *To delete slides, highlight them in the Outline view by clicking on either the box by the slide number, or any part of the text. Right-click to reveal a pop-up menu, and then select 'Delete Slide'. Alternatively, you can go to 'Edit' on the main menu bar, and select 'Delete Slide' there. The other way that you can delete a slide is to select the 'Slide Sorter' view via 'View' on the main menu bar, or by selecting the icon with four little boxes on it. You will then get an overview of all of the slides in your presentation. Simply click on the desired slide you wish to delete to highlight it, then right-click and select 'Delete Slide'.*

4. *To add slides, it is a similar process to deleting except rather than selecting 'Delete Slide', you select 'New Slide'.*

5. *To alter the Design template, go to the pull-down menu 'Format' and select 'Slide Design', as described in Activity 8.2.*

6. *Save your amended presentation under a different name by going to 'Save As...' from the 'File' pull-down menu.*

7. *To print handouts, go to 'Print' from the 'File' pull-down menu and select 'Handouts' and the number of slides to a page. Click on 'OK'.*

Activity 8.5   Printing handouts with notes

1. *Open PowerPoint by double-clicking on the icon. Open an existing presentation by clicking on the 'Open' icon.*

2. *In order to add explanatory notes to a slide, work in the 'Normal' view. This is the view where you have the 'Outline' on the left, the slide as the main part of the screen, and a notes box underneath it.*

3. *Click on the 'Notes' box and add your notes.*

4. *In order to include date/page no./title etc on the handouts, you will need to select 'View' from the main menu bar, then 'Header and Footer' and a box will appear as in Figure A.22.*

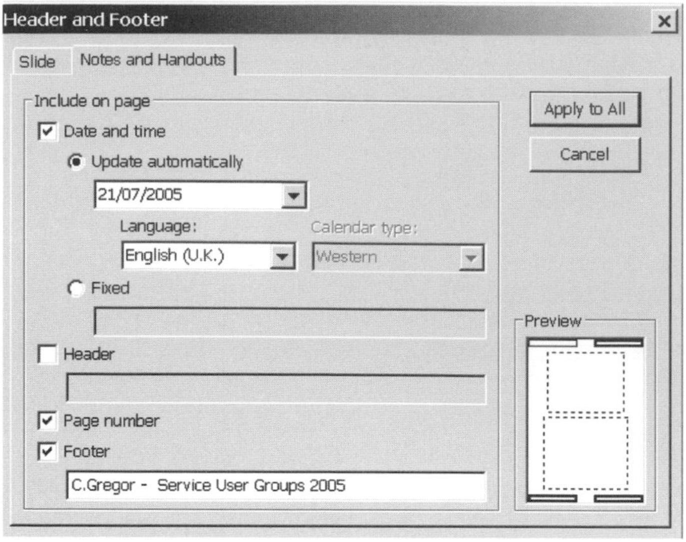

Figure A.22

Select 'Notes and Handouts' and enter the required information and then click on 'Apply to All'. This box can also be used if you wish to number your actual slides.

5. *To include these notes in handouts, select 'Print' from the 'File' pull-down menu, then 'Notes Pages' and 'OK'.*

Activity 8.6   *Using special effects*

1. *Open PowerPoint by double-clicking on the icon. Either open an existing presentation by clicking on the 'Open folder' icon or start to create a new presentation.*

2. *To add transitional effects, highlight the slide that you wish to work on. Go to 'Slide Show' from the pull-down menu. Select 'Slide Transition' and you will then get offered a range of options in the pane on the right-hand side of the screen.*

3. *Click on the transition that you would like to apply and, providing that the 'AutoPreview' box is ticked, you will be able to view the effect before committing yourself to it. You can apply the effect to all of the slides (which looks more professional and slick) or you can repeat the above steps for each slide. Once you are happy with the effects, return to the first slide and click on 'Slide Show'. Use the mouse to progress the show.*

4. *To create effects for each individual line, highlight the lines that you wish to work with, e.g. the main body of the slide. Go to 'Slide Show' from the pull-down menu and select 'Custom Animation'. Click on 'Add Effect'. Select any of the options on offer, e.g. Entrance, Fly-in.*

5. *You will then see a box appear with the lines of your text within it. There will be the icon of a mouse with a number 1 next to it. This indicates that with one click all of your highlighted text will be subject to the effect. If you wish each line to be affected, e.g. each line to 'spiral in' on the click on a mouse, click on the toggle arrow. Select 'Start on click' (see Figure A.23).*

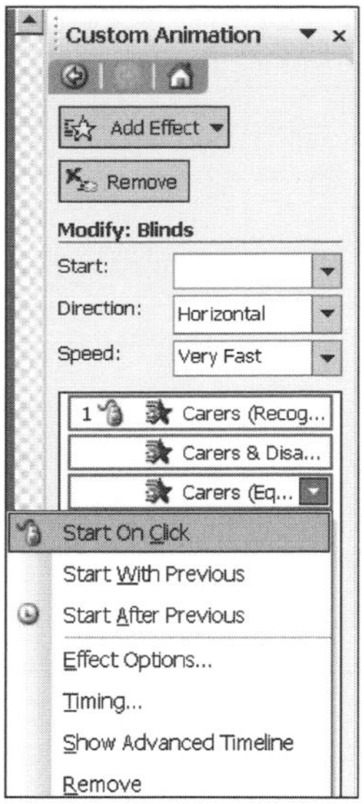

Figure A.23

You will now see a mouse and number next to each line. Click on 'Slide Show' to view the effects.

6. *Close the 'Custom Animation' pane. If you wish to view your slideshow again, go to 'Slideshow' from the pull-down menu and select 'View Show'. Click with your mouse, or use the arrow key to progress through the presentation.*

7. *Save by clicking on the 'Save' icon.*

Activity 8.7 Creating a slideshow

This is an excellent function to use if you wish to e-mail someone a PowerPoint presentation, but are unsure as to whether or not they have the software to run it. By creating a 'Slideshow' the presentation can run independently of PowerPoint.

1. *Open PowerPoint by double-clicking on the icon. Go to 'File' and then 'Save As...' to save your presentation.*

2. *Go to 'Format' from the pull-down menu and select 'Slide Design'. Chose a design template (as outlined in Activity 8.2).*

3. *In order to add transitional effects to the presentation, add your text first to the slides and then follow the steps as outlined in Activity 8.6.*

4. *To ensure that the slides run without the prompting of a mouse click, remain within the 'Slide Transitions' pane and remove the tick from the box under 'Advance Slide' that says 'Mouse Click'. Tick 'Automatically' and use the toggle keys to enter a time into the box, e.g. 10 seconds. Click on 'Apply to All Slides'.*

5. *Click on 'Slide Show' and you should be able to watch your presentation without needing to prompt the slide change.*

6. *To save as a stand-alone presentation, go to 'File' and 'Save As...' Rather than saving it as 'Presentation' (*.ppt), scroll through the types and select 'PowerPoint Show' (*.pps). Click on 'Save'.*

7. *Open up your e-mail account. Create a new e-mail to a friend and attach the PowerPoint show. Remember to ask your friend in the e-mail for feedback on whether the show worked without them having to open PowerPoint!*

Activity 8.8   Creating a greetings card using PowerPoint

1. *Open PowerPoint by double-clicking on the icon. Go to 'File' and click on 'Save As...'. Save your card/presentation.*

2. *To achieve the portrait view in PowerPoint, go to 'File' and then 'Page Setup'. A pop-up box will appear. Click on the button next to 'portrait'. Click on 'OK'.*

3. *To alter the slide format to a completely blank slide, go to the 'Format' pull-down menu and select 'Slide Layout'. Select a blank content layout from the pane on the right by clicking once on it. If there are no gridlines visible, go to 'View' from the pull-down menu, then 'Grid and Guidelines' and tick 'Display Grid'.*

4. *To type onto this, you need to create some text boxes. Go to the 'Insert' pull-down menu and select 'Text box'. Alternatively, click on the 'Text box' icon on the bottom toolbar. You will now have an uneven cross for your cursor. Place the horizontal part of the cross in the position where you want the top left-hand corner of your text box to be. Click and drag your cursor to create a text box.*

5. *Type directly into your text box. To alter the font, highlight the text and then use the relevant font icons on the toolbar.*

6. *To rotate the text by 180°, right-click to bring up the pop-up menu. Select 'Format Text box'. From the pop-up box that then appears, click on 'Size' and then type 180 into the rotation box. Click on 'OK'. Your text should now be upside down.*

7. *Draw another text box as per step 4. Click on the WordArt icon on the bottom toolbar to insert WordArt, or click on the 'Insert' pull-down menu and select 'Picture' and then 'WordArt' (see Activity 5.2 for further help).*

8. *Repeat to insert ClipArt.*

9. *Create one final text box. In order to locate the © symbol, you need to go to 'Insert' and 'Symbol' and scroll through the options until you locate it. Highlight it and then click on 'Insert'. Close the box by either clicking on X or 'Close'.*

10. *Click on the 'Print' icon. Save by clicking on the 'Save' icon.*

Activity 9.1   Filling in an online form

1. *Open Internet Explorer and type in **www.communitycare.co.uk**. Click on 'Go' or hit the Return key.*

2. *You will then be directed to the Community Care Magazine website. Scroll to the bottom of the screen and click on 'Subscribe'.*

3. *A new window will then appear. Click on 'Subscribe Free'.*

4. *A form will then appear. To complete the form, place your cursor in the first box and then click. Type in the relevant information and click on the 'Tab' button to move between boxes (clicking on 'Enter' will false-trigger the form to think that you've completed all the boxes).*

5. *At the end, click on 'Submit'.*

Activity 9.2   *Using a search engine*

1. *Open Internet Explorer and type in* **www.google.co.uk** *into the toolbar at the top of the screen. Click on 'Go' or hit the 'Return' key.*

2. *You will then be directed to the Google home page. You will then see the cursor flashing in a 'Search' box. Type in relevant key words such as 'BSL' or 'British Sign Language' and click on 'Google Search'. You should then get a number of 'hits' appearing and will need to scroll through them to see which ones are relevant for you.*

3. *A user-friendly clip-art version demonstrating finger spelling can be found at:*
   www.british-sign.co.uk/learnbslsignlanguage/fs2clipart.htm

4. *A visual dictionary comprising video clips can be found at:*
   www.british-sign.co.uk/learnbslsignlanguage/school.htm

5. *Sign language courses can be found either by searching under 'Adult Education' courses linked to your local area or by going to either the CACDP website (course examiners for BSL) or a site such as:*
   www.waterfallrainbows.co.uk/learnbslsignlanguage/findcourse/

6. *To print search results, click on the 'Print' icon on the toolbar.*

Activity 9.3   *Sending an e-mail with an attachment*

1. *Open Outlook by double-clicking on the icon.*

2. *Click on 'New' from the toolbar, or select 'New' then 'New Message' from the 'File' pull-down menu.*

3. *A blank message will then appear. Type the name of the recipient in the 'To' bar. In order to flag the message as high priority, click on the exclamation mark icon on the toolbar.*

4. *Move the cursor to the subject bar and type in a suitable subject title.*

5. *Move the cursor to the main message box and type in the message. To spell check, highlight all of the text and then click on the 'Tools' pull-down menu and select 'Spelling'.*

6. *To attach a document, go to the 'Insert' pull-down menu and select 'File'. Alternatively, click on the paperclip icon on the toolbar. You will then need to select the relevant Word document from the pop-up menu that will appear. Once you have selected your document from the options on offer, click on 'Insert'. You will then return to your e-mail and will see a Word icon and the name of your document, either at the bottom of your e-mail message, or embedded in the middle of the text. If you wish to alter its position in your e-mail, click and drag the icon to where you wish it to be positioned. Then release the mouse button.*

7. *To send the e-mail, click on 'Send'.*

Activity 9.4 — Inserting a hyperlink

1. Open Internet Explorer and type in **www.google.co.uk** into the address bar. Click on 'Go' or hit the Return key.

2. Then type a topic of interest into the blank box below the Google icon, e.g. 'government policy learning disability'. Click on 'Google Search' and a new screen will appear with relevant sites listed.

3. Click on the name of the site, which will be underlined. You will then be redirected to the website.

4. In order to send the full URL (web address) to someone else, go to the address bar and highlight the address. You can do this by simply right-clicking with the mouse over the address. A pop-up menu will then appear. Select 'Copy'.

5. Now open up your e-mail package. Create a new e-mail as above.

6. In the main text of the e-mail, 'paste' your URL by right-clicking and clicking on 'Paste' from the pop-up menu that appears.

7. Send the e-mail to your friend.

Activity 9.5 — Using the Internet

1. Open Internet Explorer and type **www.vts.rdn.ac.uk/tutorial/social-worker** into the address bar. Click on 'Go' or hit the Return key.

2. Follow the on-screen instructions. The section on Quality is within the 'Review' part of the website (the URL for p3 of Quality is **www.vts.rdn.ac.uk/tutorial/social-worker?sid=6364190&op=preview&manifestid=97&itemid=8855**).

3. When you get 'Quality 3/3 Where?' click on the 'Print' icon to print out the page.

Activity 9.6 — Contributing to an online discussion board

1. Open Internet Explorer. Type **www.socialwork-students.com/index.php** into the address bar.

2. To add the site to your favourites, click on 'Favorites'. A new pane will appear to the left of the web page. Click on 'Add' and a pop-up box will appear with the name of the web page already entered into it. You can alter this if you wish. When you are happy with the name, click on 'OK'. The hotlink to the website will then appear at the bottom of the list of 'Favorites'. In future, if you click on 'Favorites' the web address is stored here and you can go quickly to the required website without having to remember or type in the address.

3. To contribute to a discussion board on this site, click on 'Forums' on the left-hand side of the screen. You will then be directed to all of the topics that are live at the time. Click on the 'Reply' button to contribute to a forum. However, you can only contribute if registered (which is free – just follow the link on the home page).

4. To print out a copy of the discussion board, click on the 'Print' icon on the toolbar.

Activity 9.7   *Downloading media clips*

1. Log on to the website given by entering it into the address bar of Internet Explorer. Click on 'Go' or hit the 'Return' key.

2. Click on 'View Interview Film'. If you have the relevant software already downloaded on your computer, the clip will start to play automatically. However, you may get taken to another webpage that asks you to select which software application you would like to use to view the film. If you do not have any of them installed on your computer, follow the instructions on this page as to how to install them.

3. In 'Interview', the interviewer makes the following discriminatory remarks or actions:

   a. He comments on the office being on the 10th floor

   b. He places the paper knife in his drawer

   c. He refers to everyone in the office being 'mad'

   d. He comments on how he has a nut allergy.

4. In 'Committee; the slogan is 'See the Person'.

5. In order to save a video clip, rather than double-clicking on 'View Interview Film', right-click to reveal a pop-up menu which will invite you to 'Save Target As'. Select this option and then save the video in your IT Skills folder.

Activity 9.8   *Saving and forwarding web-based information*

1. Log on to the website given and complete the form.

2. In order to e-mail the completed form, highlight it and then right click to 'copy' it. You can then paste it into an e-mail by immediately going to a new e-mail and right-clicking on 'paste' in the main body of the e-mail.

3. If you wish to forward the website (which won't then include the completed form), highlight the site address at the top of the screen. Right click to copy, and then paste into an e-mail.